AF480205

THE NEW USA

WINNING THE WORLD!

YASEVA

Contents

Preface

A New Dawn for a Timeless Nation

THE NEW USA is not just another book; it is an event, an epic of monumental proportions that has emerged like a phoenix from the ashes of complacency. Rarely does such a work transcend the ordinary to shape the very fabric of a nation. Set in the present era, in the heart of America—the United States, the unparalleled beacon of power, wealth, and influence—this book arrives at a pivotal moment in history.

America, the nation where trends are set and the world follows, is now at the cusp of a transformative election—a cauldron of change, where the destiny of the country hangs in the balance. Within the pages of this majestic work, readers are taken on a journey that begins in the heavens, descends to the earth, and zeroes in on the very core of American society. It examines, critiques, and ultimately seeks to heal the nation's deepest wounds through the power of joy—a divine force capable of rectifying the world's most profound anomalies.

THE NEW USA envisions a United States reborn, setting a benchmark for all nations to follow. It tells the tale of a mighty rising, carried forward by those who embody unconditional love and the spirit of Yeshua—the selfless leaders who will usher in a reign of peace and joy that will never end. This is the new USA, a country reimagined and reinvigorated by those who take governance upon their shoulders with a commitment to justice, love, and eternal hope.

The launch of this book will be nothing short of legendary, in the presence of none other than RFK Jr., the presidential candidate destined to usher the United States into a new era, alongside his Vice Presidential candidate, the dynamic, illustrious, and visionary entrepreneur Nicole Shannon . This book actualizes the vision and mission of these two dynamic leaders, with a clear blueprint and roadmap for the future. The launch event is slated to coincide with the Feast of Michael the Archangel—a symbol of new beginnings., Heralding the birth of "The New USA' .

Prologue

The Dance of Joy

In the human journey, we often find ourselves in pursuit of happiness, that glittering treasure that promises personal satisfaction and pleasure. It is a pursuit that is self-focused, an inward gaze that seeks to fill the empty spaces within us. Happiness, however, is a creature of circumstance; its wings fragile and easily broken by the winds of change. It is a flicker of light that brightens our hearts for a moment, yet just as easily, it fades, leaving us in the shadow of what once was. In its fleeting nature, happiness can be selfish, a solitary dance that revolves around our own desires, tethered to the impermanence of life's external conditions.

But there exists a deeper, more enduring experience that transcends the limitations of happiness—a state that flows not from the well of self, but from the river of connection to others. This is joy, a boundless and selfless energy that extends beyond the confines of our individual lives. Joy is others-focused, born from compassion, love, and a profound sense of belonging to the tapestry of humanity. It is a flame that burns not just for ourselves, but for the well-being and happiness of those around us, illuminating the path with a light that does not dim.

Unlike happiness, joy is limitless. It does not hinge on the shifting sands of our circumstances, nor is it subject to the whims of our personal satisfaction. Instead, joy is an ever-present force, rooted in the understanding that we are all connected, that our lives are intertwined in ways that are both beautiful and mysterious. It is in this interconnectedness that joy finds its strength, offering us a sense of fulfilment that is not only profound but enduring.

To embrace joy is to expand our circle of concern beyond ourselves, to allow our hearts to stretch wide with empathy and understanding. It encourages us to act with kindness, to engage in selfless acts that ripple outward, touching the lives of others in ways we may never fully comprehend. Joy, in its purest form, creates a sense of unity, a bond that transcends the barriers of self-centeredness and unites us in a common humanity.

In this way, joy becomes a source of inspiration and strength, not just for ourselves, but for others as well. It is a beacon that guides us through the trials and tribulations of life, reminding us that our greatest fulfilment lies not in what we can take, but in what we can give. Joy is the song that resonates within our souls, echoing through the corridors of time, a melody of love, connection, and enduring grace.

As you turn the pages of this book, may you find not just the pursuit of happiness, but the deeper, more enriching journey towards joy. Let these words be a reminder that while happiness may dance in and out of our lives, it is joy that remains steadfast and true, lighting our way with a warmth that no darkness can extinguish.

Happiness is self-focused and therefore gets limited.

Joy, on the other hand, is others-focused and therefore is limitless.

Yaseva - Founder of Joyism

CHAPTER ONE

The land of milk and honey... of technology and luxury

Section 1

Celestial Introduction

In the annals of American history, many significant events have shaped the nation's identity, but few are as profoundly symbolic as the decision made in 1955 when President Isova of the United States enshrined the phrase "In God We Trust" upon the nation's currency. This seemingly simple act, embedding divine reverence on every note, every dollar that passes through countless hands, carries a weight far beyond its physical form. It is a testament to a nation's collective faith, a beacon that illuminates the enduring connection between the temporal and the eternal.

This sacred inscription, unknown to most in its celestial significance, reverberates not just within the boundaries of human understanding but reaches the very heights of the heavens themselves. It is a declaration, a covenant of trust between a people and their Creator, one that the heavens have long cherished and celebrated with unparalleled grandeur. Every year, on the Fourth of July, as the earthly realm commemorates its independence, the heavens engage in a celebration of divine trust that surpasses all human comprehension.

Imagine, if you will, a scene of unimaginable splendour and grandeur, where the heavens unfurl their most resplendent colours, a tapestry of hues and depths that extend far beyond the horizons of our mortal gaze, nearly touching the very edges of eternity. This celestial spectacle is not merely a sight to behold but an all-encompassing experience—a panorama of divine artistry that envelops all within its embrace, forming a globe of visual magnificence that transcends the limitations of earthly senses.

At the heart of this divine pageantry stands the Almighty in His infinite splendour, surrounded by the host of heaven—the angels, the sons of God, and other exalted beings whose nature and origins lie beyond the Angelic Realm. Even the forces of darkness, the minions of Satan and Satan himself, are drawn to this grand splendour, compelled to witness the Almighty's glory and the enduring faith of a nation that dares to inscribe its trust in the Divine upon its currency.

As this celestial celebration moves on, a hush falls over the assembled hosts. The first Angel, radiant and majestic, rises from among the throngs, ready to announce a proclamation that echoes through the cosmos, reverberating in the hearts of all who have the privilege to hear. This moment, filled with profound anticipation, marks the beginning of a narrative that transcends time and space, a story of divine trust, human faith, and the cosmic significance of a nation's pledge to the Almighty.

Michael – The Leader of the Archangels, Protector of the Faithful: The Titan of Economy

With the force of a celestial storm, I, Michael, the leader of the archangels, proclaim the unmatched power of America's economic engine. It is a roaring titan, a machine of divine creation, honed to perfection in the forge of capitalism. The United States stands as a beacon, its economy pulsating with the energy of innovation and enterprise. In this land, wealth is not merely amassed—it is divinely crafted, fuelling a cycle of prosperity that propels America to the zenith of global economic power. The fruits of this nation's labour are the envy of the world, a testament to the righteous path of free enterprise that I, as protector, guard with unwavering vigilance.

Gabriel – The Messenger of God, Announcer of the Incarnation: High Standard of Living

As the messenger of divine truths, I, Gabriel, herald the reality of America's unparalleled standard of living—a reality that echoes through the heavens. In this blessed land, the pursuit of happiness is not a mere declaration but a divine promise fulfilled. The cities of America hum with life, where comfort and luxury are the birthrights of its people. From the sprawling suburbs to the vibrant metropolises, the American Dream is a living testament to the power of determination and faith. It is I, Gabriel, who declares this truth: in America, the good life is not a privilege for the few but a promise extended to all who seek it.

Raphael – The Healer, Restorer of Sight and Health: Global Power

In the name of healing and restoration, I, Raphael, bear witness to America's global power—an influence that extends like a healing balm across the world. Just as I restore health and sight, America restores balance and order on the global stage. Like the mighty eagle, America's influence soars above the earth, its power felt in every corner of the globe. As the unrivalled superpower, the United States stands as a bulwark against tyranny, a defender of freedom, and a beacon of hope. The American ideal, guided by divine wisdom, shapes the destiny of nations, ensuring that justice and liberty reign supreme.

Uriel – The Illuminator, Bringer of Knowledge and Wisdom: Technology

I, Uriel, the bringer of knowledge and wisdom, illuminate the path of technological advancement that America treads with divine purpose. In the crucible of American ingenuity, technology is forged into the tools that shape the future of mankind. Here, in the land of invention, the impossible is made possible, and the wonders of the digital age are brought to life. From Silicon Valley to the laboratories of the nation's greatcst minds, America leads the charge in the global tech race. It is through the divine illumination I provide that the United States remains the undisputed leader, setting trends and standards that the world follows with reverence.

Selaphiel – The Prayerful Intercessor, Guardian of the Prayers of the Faithful: Wealth

As the guardian of prayers, I, Selaphiel, lift up the supplications of the faithful, ensuring that the wealth of America is both a blessing and a responsibility. America's riches, vast and multifaceted, are the modern-day treasures of a new world, unlocked by the industriousness of its people. This wealth is not hoarded; it is distributed across a dynamic and diverse economy, reflecting the divine promise that all who come to America's shores can share in its bounty. I, Selaphiel, ensure that these prayers of prosperity are heard, that the nation's affluence continues to be a testament to its enduring promise.

Jegudiel – The Protector of the Faithful, Bringer of Mercy and Forgiveness: Education

In the name of mercy and forgiveness, I, Jegudiel, protect the faithful as they pursue the light of knowledge in America's hallowed institutions. Education in this land is both a lighthouse and a fortress, guiding and protecting the minds of the future. From the ivory towers of renowned universities to the classrooms where curiosity is nurtured, America's commitment to education is a pathway to greatness. As the protector of the faithful, I ensure that the seeds of knowledge sown in this land bear fruit, that the torch of wisdom burns brightly, lighting the way for generations to come.

Barachiel – The Blessed Messenger, Bringer of Blessings and Joy: Space Exploration

As the harbinger of blessings and joy, I, Barachiel, celebrate America's celestial achievements—its ascent to the stars, where greatness knows no bounds. Among the cosmos, America's pioneering spirit reaches its zenith, leading the charge into the final frontier. NASA, a symbol of American ingenuity and determination, turns dreams into reality, exploring the vastness of space with the same fervour that drives the nation's quest for excellence on Earth. The rockets that pierce the heavens are more than vessels of exploration; they are symbols of America's boundless ambition, a reflection of the divine blessings that I, Barachiel, shower upon this great nation.

The Everlasting Glory

Together, as the heavenly hosts, we proclaim the everlasting glory of America—a nation whose greatness is a multifaceted jewel, each facet reflecting the brilliance of its economy, the comfort of its standard of living, the reach of its global power, the marvel of its technology, the abundance of its wealth, the enlightenment of its education, and the boundless possibilities of its space exploration. This is a nation that not only achieves greatness but defines it, setting the standard by which all others are measured. As the world watches, America continues its majestic ascent, a colossus that strides confidently into the future, its greatness undiminished and its promise eternal. We, the archangels, stand in awe and support, forever glorifying the land that embodies the virtues we so fiercely protect and cherish.

Michael – The Path Forward: A Celestial Mandate for America

In the name of the Almighty, I, Michael, the Leader of the Archangels and Protector of the Faithful, speak of a nation that stands at a pivotal moment in its divine journey. The United States, a land forged by the hands of the brave and the hearts of the just, is now at a crossroads. The future that unfolds before us is not merely one of continued ascent and triumph but one of deep reflection and righteous struggle.

America, you have been bestowed with unparalleled greatness—a beacon of freedom, prosperity, and innovation in a world often shrouded in darkness. Yet, with this divine gift comes the weighty responsibility of moral and spiritual stewardship. Your greatness is not a guarantee of infallibility, nor is it a shield against the trials that test the soul of your nation. As you stride confidently into the future, you must confront the shadows that linger within your borders—the shadows of inequality, injustice, and division that threaten to undermine the very foundation upon which your greatness stands.

This is not just a tale of victory, but of vigilance. It is a narrative that demands you to reflect upon the moral dilemmas that challenge your unity and to address the societal issues that call for resolution. Your path forward is clear: the pursuit of continued greatness must be tempered with the divine principles of justice, equality, and compassion. These are not mere virtues to be admired from afar but imperatives to be enacted in every corner of your land.

America, you are a nation at a crossroads, where every decision you make, every action you take, carries with it the weight of your destiny and the destiny of the world that looks to you for guidance. The crossroads before you is not just a choice between paths but a test of your moral compass. Will you continue to ascend, not just in power and influence, but in righteousness and virtue? Or will you falter, allowing the shadows within to cloud your vision and weaken your resolve?

The true measure of your greatness lies not in the accolades of the past or the power you wield, but in your ability to overcome the challenges that test your soul. It is in your response to these trials that your legacy will be written. The world watches, not just for your leadership in times of prosperity, but for your courage in the face of adversity, your commitment to justice in the midst of strife, and your compassion in the presence of suffering.

Be known that your journey is far from over. The path you choose will determine not only your future but the future of all who seek refuge and inspiration in the light you cast. I, Michael, stand as your protector, urging you to rise above the challenges that lie ahead with the strength and righteousness that have always been your guiding stars. Let your actions be a testament to the divine purpose that has been entrusted to you, and may you continue to stride confidently into the future, with your greatness undiminished and your soul unyielding in the pursuit of justice, equality, and compassion.

A Divine Perspective: The Challenge of Morality

Yet, even as America ascends, a celestial dialogue reveals the challenges that accompany such greatness. In a conversation between God and Satan, the moral and spiritual state of the United States is put under intense scrutiny. God, fully aware of the nation's declaration of trust in Him, poses a question to Satan: "Have you considered, a nation that proudly proclaims 'In God We Trust' on its currency, is home to three Christian candidates for the presidency?"

Satan, with his characteristic cynicism, challenges this notion of righteousness. With a cryptic and cynical snigger, he highlights the mire into which the nation has sunk, despite its outward professions of faith.

With a dark and malevolent satisfaction, Satan summons his minions to reveal their maliciousness, causing the societal decay and moral failings that now plague the United States, the favoured nation of God.

One by one, the demons reveal a different aspect of America's struggles:

Beelzebub speaks of the deep roots of racial and ethnic inequality, where systemic racism flourishes and division grows. Despite protests and cries for justice, the cycle of violence and despair continues, fuelled by justified brutality and profiling.

Mammon gloats over the widening chasm between rich and poor. The wealth of the nation pools in the hands of a few, while the homeless wander the streets of the richest cities, ignored and forgotten. Job insecurity ravages the working class, leaving many desperate and without hope.

Asmodeus revels in the twisted desires that have corrupted the healthcare system, where greed bleeds the system dry, leaving millions without care. The opioid crisis, unchecked and unchallenged, devastates communities, a plague upon the land.

Belial manipulates the value of education, ensuring that the rich are lavished with resources while the poor struggle under crumbling institutions. Students are shackled with debt, a burden that crushes their future before it even begins.

Mephistopheles boasts of the battlefield he has made of politics. Misinformation spreads like wildfire, deepening divides that may never heal. Trust in institutions crumbles daily as partisanship stokes debates that are venomous and futile.

Astaroth sows discord among the sexes, ensuring that gender inequality prevails. Women continue to earn less and fight harder for basic rights, while workplaces remain battlegrounds of respect, where harassment and assault are drowned out by the noise of injustice.

Baal unleashes war through the nation's adoration of guns. Mass shootings have become routine, tearing families apart as debates over rights only serve to bring more death. The streets of America have become battlegrounds where the innocent are caught in the crossfire.

Leviathan unleashes the fury of the earth, accelerating climate change and bringing storms, fires, and floods that devastate the poor and vulnerable. No corner of the country is spared from the relentless assault of natural disasters.

Azazel spreads hatred against LGBTQ+ individuals, ensuring that discrimination is rampant and violence is often ignored or justified. The struggle for equality is steeped in blood, shadowed by whispers of bigotry and prejudice.

A Moment of Divine Reflection

Satan, pleased with the chaos and despair his minions have sown, revels in the turmoil. "See, O almighty, the nation that professes to trust in You, in reality, struggles under the weight of its moral failings and societal challenges; frayed and weakened by my devoted forces of darkness." Satan lets go a sickening and horrible laugh.

God, fully aware of all that transpires, closes His eyes and turns away, saddened. The angels, witnessing the unfolding emotions, are thrown into a state of panic, unsure of what the future holds. But then, with a decisive gesture, God snaps His fingers, and in an instant, Michael the Archangel steps forward. He shuts down the entire spectacle, sending the spiritual beings away with a command: "The show is over. Go back."

Satan and his demons, though momentarily seem triumphant, are dismissed from the divine presence. They leave with howling laughter, satisfied with the seeds of chaos they have sown.

Section 2: The Council of the Celestial Hosts

Amidst the resplendent halls of the heavenly realms, where light cascaded like waterfalls of purest gold and the very air thrummed with divine purpose, Archangel Michael, the stalwart leader of the celestial legions, convened a council of utmost gravity. The United States, once the shining city upon a hill, now found itself engulfed in shadows that threatened to obscure its beacon of hope. The gathering of the most senior angels—the illustrious leaders of the heavenly hosts—was a moment of unparalleled significance, for they were tasked with discerning the root causes of the dire state that beset the nation.

As the luminous beings assembled, their countenances, ordinarily serene and radiant, were etched with concern. Each angel bore the weight of celestial wisdom, yet their thoughts were clouded by the uncertainties of the mortal world below.

"It is the insidious lure of Mammon—the voracious spirit of greed—that has ensnared humanity," declared one angel, his voice resonant with the authority of aeons. His accusation was directed at the dark force that had tightened its grip on the hearts of men, leading them astray in their pursuit of wealth.

"But what of the devout Christians?" countered another, his tone laden with a mix of sorrow and bewilderment. "What have they been doing, if not standing as bulwarks against this moral decay?"

"And the priests and bishops, those anointed as shepherds of the flock?" a third angel queried, his wings trembling with righteous indignation. "Surely, they should have been the first to rise against this tide of darkness, to illuminate the path with their unwavering faith."

"What of the countless congregations of priests and nuns?" echoed a fourth, his voice tinged with a note of despair. "Are they not the hands and feet of divine intervention? Why have they not stemmed the flow of corruption?"

"And the myriad Christian institutions of higher learning?" interjected another angel, his eyes burning with the light of divine knowledge. "Where are their voices in these tumultuous times? Why have they not wielded the sword of truth against the falsehoods that plague the land?"

Then, a voice, trembling with near desperation, pierced the charged atmosphere. "And the seminaries, those hallowed grounds where priests are instructed in the sacred mysteries—what are they doing? Why has their influence not been felt in a world so desperately in need of spiritual guidance?"

The chamber, filled with the light of a thousand suns, now reverberated with the sound of accusations as each angel sought to pinpoint the failing that had led to the present calamity. The din of divine debate reached a crescendo, threatening to fracture the very harmony of the celestial spheres.

But before the cacophony could spiral into discord, Archangel Michael, his presence commanding and his gaze unwavering, raised his hand. Instantly, a profound silence descended upon the assembly, as if the universe itself held its breath.

"Enough!" Michael's voice, imbued with the authority of Heaven itself, rang out like a clarion call. "Cease this blame game at once!"

The angels, their luminous forms stilled, turned their full attention to Michael, the protector of the faithful and the bearer of Heaven's sword.

"Look not to the past with recrimination," Michael continued, his tone now firm yet laced with compassion. "Instead, behold the reality before us. It is election time in the world's greatest nation—an era of decision and destiny. What is the change that can happen? What are the fractures that must be healed, and how can we, as the agents of the Divine, support that transformation? Let us not dwell on what has been lost, but rather focus on what can be restored. We must move forward, illuminating the path that lies ahead."

With this directive, the angels, their wings unfurling as if ready to soar into action, turned their gaze upon the Earth, in deep contemplation. Each angel, a paragon of divine wisdom, identified one critical issue after another that plagued the United States, offering their celestial insight into the

As the leader of the archangels and the vigilant guardian of the faithful, Michael was the first to speak. His voice, resonant with the weight of his station, echoed through the chamber. "The United States is scarred by deep-seated racial and ethnic inequalities," he proclaimed. "These wounds manifest in the form of systemic racism, mass incarceration, and a profound lack of trust between law enforcement and the communities they serve. To heal these divisions, we must advocate for comprehensive criminal justice reform, promote anti-racism education across all levels of society, and invest in economic empowerment for marginalised groups. Only by addressing these injustices can the nation begin to rebuild trust and unity, restoring the bonds that once held it together."

Next to step forward was Gabriel, the divine messenger and the herald of the Incarnation. His words carried the weight of divine decree. "Economic inequality is a blight upon the soul of the nation," he declared with unwavering conviction. "The chasm between the rich and the poor continues to widen, eroding the very foundations of society. To bridge this divide, we must champion progressive taxation, ensure that every worker receives a living wage, and consider the implementation of a Universal Basic Income to provide a safety net for the most vulnerable. By addressing these economic disparities, we can restore hope and dignity to all citizens, ensuring that the promise of prosperity is not an empty one."

Raphael, the healer and restorer of health, spoke with a voice suffused with compassion and wisdom. "The American healthcare system is in dire need of reform," he intoned. "Millions languish without access to adequate care, and the opioid crisis ravages communities, leaving devastation in its wake. A move towards universal healthcare is not merely a necessity but a moral imperative, ensuring that every individual, regardless of their station, can receive the care they need. Furthermore, expanding mental health services and addressing the opioid epidemic with comprehensive treatment programmes are crucial steps in healing the nation, both in body and in spirit."

Uriel, the illuminator and bringer of divine knowledge, turned his piercing gaze towards the nation's educational system. "Education is the key to unlocking a prosperous future," he began, his voice a beacon of clarity. "Yet the system is riddled with inequities that threaten to derail the dreams of the young. Schools in impoverished communities are starved of resources, and the burden of student debt weighs heavily on the shoulders of those who seek to better themselves. We must reform school funding models to ensure fairness, make higher education more affordable, and invest in early childhood education to close the achievement gaps. In doing so, we unlock the boundless potential that lies within every student, securing the future of the nation."

Selaphiel, the prayerful intercessor and guardian of the faithful's prayers, addressed the deepening chasm of political polarisation. His voice, a calming balm, sought to soothe the rifts that threatened to tear the nation asunder. "Political polarisation has reached perilous levels," he warned, his tone both grave and hopeful. "The nation is splintered into factions, each entrenched in its own beliefs, refusing to listen to the other. This discord sows chaos and undermines the very fabric of democracy. To heal these divisions, we must promote civic education that encourages critical thinking, foster bipartisan collaboration in legislative halls, and implement media literacy programmes to counter the pernicious spread of misinformation. Only through understanding and dialogue can we bridge the divides and restore unity to the nation."

Jegudiel, the protector of the faithful and the harbinger of mercy and forgiveness, turned the discussion to the pressing issue of gender equality. His voice, a blend of stern resolve and compassionate advocacy, echoed through the hall. "Despite the strides made, women continue to face significant challenges in the workplace and in society at large," he observed with a tone that brooked no denial. "The gender pay gap remains a stark reality, and gender-based violence is a scourge that must be eradicated. We must strengthen pay equity legislation, expand support for working families, and increase funding for programmes that combat domestic violence and sexual assault. In doing so, we affirm the dignity and worth of all individuals, ensuring that every person, regardless of gender, is treated with the respect they deserve."

Barachiel, the blessed messenger and bringer of divine blessings and joy, approached the issue of gun violence with solemnity. "The epidemic of gun violence in the United States is a tragedy that can no longer be ignored," he declared, his voice heavy with sorrow and determination. "To confront this crisis, we must implement comprehensive gun control measures, including universal background checks and red flag laws. Additionally, we must invest in community violence prevention programmes and treat gun violence as the public health issue it truly is. By employing data-driven strategies, we can protect lives and restore peace to communities torn apart by senseless acts of violence."

Suriel, the angel of healing, turned his attention to the Earth itself, the cradle of humanity. "The United States bears a great responsibility to address the looming threat of climate change and to protect the environment," he proclaimed, his voice resonant with the gravity of the task. "The effects of environmental degradation are most acutely felt by the poor and vulnerable, who suffer disproportionately from the consequences of pollution and climate-related disasters. We must advocate for transformative policies, such as the Green New Deal, strengthen environmental regulations to safeguard our natural resources, and invest in climate adaptation strategies. Protecting the Earth is not only a matter of justice but a sacred duty to future generations."

Raguel, the angel of justice and fairness, cast his gaze upon the marginalised and oppressed. "Discrimination and violence against LGBTQ+ individuals are blights upon the conscience of the nation," he asserted, his voice ringing with the authority of divine judgement. "We must strengthen and enforce anti-discrimination laws, support the rights of transgender individuals, and promote inclusivity in education. By doing so, we ensure that all people, regardless of their sexual orientation or gender identity, are treated with the dignity and respect that is their due. Justice demands nothing less."

Lastly, Zadkiel, the angel of mercy and freedom, spoke of the vital importance of community and civic engagement. His voice, gentle yet resolute, called the assembly to action. "A thriving democracy depends on the active participation of its citizens," he reminded the gathering. "We must support grassroots movements that work to address social inequalities, foster public-private partnerships to tackle the nation's most pressing issues, and encourage civic participation through voter registration drives and advocacy training. By empowering communities and giving a voice to the marginalised, we can strengthen the very fabric of society and build a more just and inclusive nation."

A profound silence settled over the celestial council. Archangel Michael, ever the vigilant leader, contemplated the enormity of the task before them. "These challenges are vast and complex," he acknowledged, his voice heavy with the weight of his charge. "Yet they are not insurmountable by the overcoming spirit of love, peace and joy. With divine guidance and the collective efforts of the faithful, the United States can rise above these trials and emerge stronger, purer, and more just."

The angels, their hearts lifted by Michael's words, prepared to return to their celestial duties. But before they departed, they joined together in a powerful chorus, a hymn to the need for God's mercy and grace in these troubled times. Their voices, a symphony of divine harmonies, echoed through the heavens, a reminder to all creation that no challenge is too great, no darkness too deep, for the light of divine providence to overcome.

As the final notes of their song faded into the infinite, Michael spoke once more. "Let us remain vigilant, my brothers and sisters. We must watch over this nation and its people, ready to guide and assist them in their time of need. The work of Providence is ongoing, and we are its instruments."

With that, the angels dispersed, their spirits buoyed by the hope that through their efforts, and the boundless mercy of God, the United States would find its way through the darkness and into the light of a new dawn.

Section 3

The Celestial Inquisition and the Quest for Divine Wisdom

In the exalted spheres of Heaven, where the divine will is deciphered and the destinies of nations are meticulously pondered, Archangel Michael found himself enveloped in deep contemplation. What had stirred the very heart of the Almighty? Why had the Lord expressed a rare and profound excitement regarding three Christian candidates vying for the presidency of the United States? How will the nation's influence reverberate across the globe, with Christianity-centred leadership to shape the course of history itself? What qualities, Michael wondered, do these three presidential candidates possess? Does it warrant divine attention?

To uncover the truth, Michael summoned three of his most trusted lieutenants—Uriel, the Illuminator and Bringer of Knowledge and Wisdom; Selaphiel, the Prayerful Intercessor and Guardian of the Prayers of the Faithful; and Jegudiel, the Protector of the Faithful and Bringer of Mercy and Forgiveness. Together, these angels would employ their celestial intelligence and unparalleled insight to scrutinise the spiritual and moral fabric of each candidate. The stakes were immense, for the outcome of their inquiry could determine the spiritual trajectory of an entire nation.

The Conundrum of Faith and Political Allegiance

The first candidate to undergo divine scrutiny was Kamala Harris. Born to a Jamaican Christian father and a Tamil Hindu mother, Harris had embraced Christianity as her faith, regularly attending a Baptist church. Yet, despite her religious affiliation, Michael and Uriel discerned a troubling paradox within her political life. As a prominent figure in the Democratic Party, Harris publicly supported abortion rights—a stance that starkly contradicted Christian doctrine, which sanctifies life from the moment of conception and condemns abortion as a grievous sin.

In their celestial inquiry, Uriel illuminated the profound conflict that raged within Harris's soul. On one hand, her faith instilled in her the belief in the sanctity of life, a core tenet of Christianity. On the other hand, her political obligations demanded that she uphold the right of women to make autonomous decisions about their bodies—a right fervently defended by many in the United States as an essential aspect of personal freedom. This clash between her spiritual beliefs and her political stance cast a long shadow over her Christian witness. The angels pondered the implications of such a compromise, questioning whether Harris's allegiance to her party had eclipsed her commitment to the eternal tenets of her faith.

The Paradox of Evangelical Rhetoric

Next, the angels turned their gaze toward Donald Trump, a candidate who boldly identified as an Evangelical Christian. Selaphiel, the Prayerful Intercessor, took the lead in delving into Trump's life, seeking the divine truth behind his public persona. Trump's vocal opposition to abortion aligned him with Christian values, particularly those cherished by the evangelical community. However, as Selaphiel and Michael probed deeper, they uncovered a disconcerting paradox that could not be ignored.

Despite his fervent claims of devout Christianity, Trump's actions often revealed a stark departure from the teachings of Christ. His harsh policies towards immigrants, marked by a lack of compassion and empathy, his inflammatory rhetoric that fuelled division and sowed discord, and his apparent disregard for the principles of love and humility painted a troubling picture. Selaphiel was particularly disturbed by Trump's ominous declaration that there would be a "bloodbath" if the Republicans lost the election—a statement that seemed to contradict the Christian call for peace, reconciliation, and the preservation of life.

The angels found themselves questioning the depth of Trump's faith, wondering whether his evangelical identity was more a matter of political expediency than genuine spiritual conviction. How could a leader who professed to follow Christ engage in actions that so blatantly contradicted the very ethos of the Gospel? This dissonance led the celestial council to consider the complexity of Trump's spiritual journey and the sincerity of his professed beliefs.

The Independent Conscience

The final candidate to be scrutinised was Robert Francis Kennedy Jr., a figure who, unlike his rivals, had chosen to run as an independent candidate, free from the constraints and dogmas of the major political parties. Jegudiel, the Bringer of Mercy and Forgiveness, took the lead in evaluating Kennedy's moral and spiritual character. Kennedy's opposition to abortion, despite his personal history of multiple marriages and divorces, reflected a commitment to certain moral principles that set him apart from the other candidates.

What intrigued Jegudiel most was Kennedy's unwavering courage to stand against powerful and entrenched interests, such as the pharmaceutical industry, and his willingness to speak truth to power regardless of the consequences. His advocacy for reducing military expenditure, his passionate defence of the environment, and his commitment to addressing climate change further underscored his dedication to justice and righteousness. Unlike the other candidates, Kennedy appeared to be guided not by political convenience but by a sincere and steadfast dedication to the common good.

The angels saw in Kennedy a reflection of the moral integrity that had characterised leaders of old, those who led not by seeking personal gain but by upholding principles that transcended their own interests. His independence from the suffocating grip of party politics allowed him to pursue a path of righteousness, unshackled by the demands of partisan loyalty. Perhaps it was this independent spirit, this unwavering commitment to truth and justice, that had captured God's attention and prompted the divine excitement.

The Will of God in Leadership

As the angels reflected on their findings, Selaphiel, ever attuned to the prayers of the faithful, offered a poignant observation. "The people have been praying in their millions for the right candidate to emerge—one who will lead with justice, righteousness, and compassion. Surely, God will answer their prayers and allow such a leader to rise."

But Michael, with the wisdom of the ages and the burden of experience, responded with a solemn reminder that shook the very foundation of their understanding. "Have you ever considered the difference between whom God would allow and whom God would want? The Almighty's will is not always fulfilled in the leaders who rise to power. Sometimes, God allows a leader to emerge, not because they are the best choice, but because they are the choice of the people—reflecting their hearts, their desires, and their flaws."

The angels were taken aback, their divine understanding deepening as they absorbed Michael's profound words. The distinction between divine allowance and divine desire was a revelation that carried immense implications. A leader whom God wanted would embody justice, righteousness, humility, and compassion, guiding the nation with integrity and an unwavering commitment to the welfare of all people. But in the absence of such leaders, God might allow others to rise. Because God can get His will done by anyone, even Satan!

The Commission to Uncover the Truth

In the wake of this revelation, the angels pondered their next course of action, sombrely flapping their wings. "What do we do now?" one of them asked, their voice tinged with both curiosity and concern. "Are we to support the candidate whom God desires, or should we seek a single solution?" Then from the group an excited voice declared, "We need someone with a panacea! One that could solve all these problems and bring peace and prosperity to the nation!""Wonderful!"Michael exclaimed in exultation! "A panacea is what we will await! Connecting with one love, one peace and one joy!

Angelic team one commissioned.

The ever decisive leader, Michael gave the angels their commission with clarity and purpose. "Go forth, Uriel and Selaphiel, and investigate the true problems that plague the United States. Look beyond the surface issues to the underlying deceptions, the sophisticated mischief, and the spread of deceit that undermines the very foundation of the nation's politics. Uncover the hidden forces at play—the syndicates, the cartels, the lobbyists, and the pervasive systemic corruption. Reveal the true state of the United States and the profound moral and spiritual challenges that lay ahead. Only by understanding the full scope of the challenges can we devise a strategy to ensure that the divine will is ultimately served. Descend into the heart of the nation's troubles, uncovering the forces that sought to manipulate and control its destiny from the shadows."

Angelic team two commissioned.

Jegudiel and Barachiel Michael said, "You may go wherever and seek out leaders who have discovered a panacea that has the potential to bring about the true transformation that is needed. Not the rabble-rousing kind! The spirit of God is sure to be working among the true seekers for sure. Go find them, in whichever nook or corner of the world they are in."Gather information about the wise and trustworthy ministers of God on earth, who have the wise actions we are seeking. The US needs special guidance, that is the desire of God," Michael said with conviction. "Whatever the outcome of the election, may the divine will of God steer the nation towards a future of righteousness and justice," Michael closed with a prayerful invocation.

The angelic teams departed, their mission clear and their resolve unshakeable. Thus, the stage was set for a twin celestial investigation from heaven to bring light to the darkness, to expose the hidden truths, and to pave the way for a 'panacea' to emerge that would guide nations with the virtues of justice, mercy, and humility, as ordained by the Almighty.

CHAPTER TWO

The Tares Among the Wheat

Section 1

With the two angelic teams gone on their crucial mission, a celestial reckoning on the anomalies of present-day visible Christianity on earth drew the attention of Michael. In the resplendent chambers of the Heavenly Council, where truth is illuminated by the purest light of divine understanding, Archangel Michael, his thoughts heavy, had been gnawing at his celestial soul. The trajectory of Christianity, from its humble origins in the dust of ancient lands to its present-day manifestation, had strayed far from the path intended by the Almighty. Michael, the warrior of Heaven, now found himself not in battle with dark forces, but in a battle for the soul of the faith itself. What had gone wrong? What forces had led the faithful so far from the teachings of Yeshua the Christ? The time had come to confront these questions with the full weight of Heaven's wisdom.

Archangel Michael stood before the assembly of divine beings. His once radiant form seemed to dim, as if burdened by the weight of what was to come. The silence in the hall was thick with anticipation, every angelic being attuned to the gravity of the moment. A Grieving Sentinel Speaks. A Lament for the Deviations of Faith

"Brothers and sisters of the celestial realm, hear me," Michael began, his voice a solemn melody of authority and sorrow. He stood not as the triumphant warrior who cast out the ancient serpent, but as a grieving sentinel. "I lament the wayward paths trodden by those who bear the name of Christ. The stewards of His message, once entrusted with preserving the sacred truth, have allowed the essence of faith to become diluted. Have they forgotten their charge?"

Michael's gaze swept across the assembly, his celestial eyes filled with sorrow. "The artisans of faith—those who paint, who sing, who craft the prayers of the faithful—have strayed far from the divine blueprint. What was once an act of worship, a reflection of God's glory, has in many cases become a distortion, a mere echo of divine intention. The imagery, the hymns, the rituals—are they still rooted in the truth, or have they become 'happy clappy' emotional, senses titillating sessions, mere shadows of what they were meant to be?"

His voice grew stronger, infused with righteous indignation. "Consider the Lord's Prayer, that sacred invocation taught by our Lord Himself: 'Our Father in heaven, hallowed be your name.' It was a prayer of longing, a plea for God's divine presence to take root on earth. But with Pentecost, when the Holy Spirit descended to dwell within every believer, a new reality dawned—God not only in heaven but within us. Yet, this profound shift has gone unrecognized, unspoken, unprayed. The prayer remains as it was, a relic of a time before the Spirit indwelt every believer, leaving the faithful with a half-spoken truth, a communion with God not fully realized."

Michael's tone shifted, sorrow mingling with disappointment. "And what of the hymns, those sacred songs meant to lift the soul to God? They are still laden with the pleas of the Old Covenant, cries that were once fitting but are now obsolete in the light of the New Covenant. 'Take not your Holy Spirit from me,' the psalmist cried, but under the New Covenant, the Spirit remains unless grievously driven away. These songs, once lifelines, have become chains, binding the faithful to a mindset of fear and uncertainty rather than leading them into the freedom and assurance Christ purchased at so great a cost."

Michael's countenance darkened as he spoke of the modern practices of worship. "The Sabbath, the day of rest ordained by God, has been cast aside, replaced by a day of worship chosen not for its holiness but for convenience. The Sabbath was a covenant, a sign between God and His people, yet it has been exchanged for a day that suits the schedules of men rather than the will of God. And what has become of worship itself? Once a sacred assembly, a gathering of hearts before their Creator, it has turned into a spectacle, a performance. Grand stages, dazzling lights, and carefully orchestrated services—these have taken the place of the humble gathering where God's presence was once palpably felt. The focus of worship has shifted from the indwelling presence of God to peculiar and trivial outward manifestations."

His voice faltered, a rare crack in his usually unyielding demeanour. "What of the mission Christ left for His followers? To do good, to heal, to set free? Many still walk this path, yes, but too many others have strayed far from it. Christians now find themselves in industries and practices that Christ would have abhorred. The pharmaceutical industry, driven by greed, not compassion, enslaves rather than heals. Manufacturing weapons, perpetuating corruption, creating systems of oppression. How did this happen? How did the people of God become entangled in the very things Christ came to destroy? This is not the work of God; it is the work of the enemy, masked as progress."

Michael stood silent for a moment, as if gathering strength for his final words. "And what of the world today?" he asked, his voice trembling with the weight of his divine sorrow. "The earth groans under the weight of humanity's sin—climate ravaged, creation corrupted. The pursuit of wealth has blinded the eyes of the wise and the powerful. The education systems, designed to enlighten, now serve to entrench the status quo, teaching not wisdom but the accumulation of wealth. The cycles of violence and oppression, which Christ came to break, are perpetuated by those who claim to follow Him. Nations that once bore the banner of Christ have become agents of destruction, leaving their people spiritually dead—alive in body, perhaps, but dead in spirit."

As he concluded, Michael's voice softened, the strength of his words now tinged with a deep, abiding sorrow. "Is this the faith that Yeshua the Messiah, the Christ, died to establish? Is this the legacy He intended for His Church? We grieve for the lost, the misguided, the deceived. But there is still hope—hope for a return to the true essence of faith, hope for a revival of the Spirit that was once so vibrantly alive within the Church. But it requires repentance, a turning back to the God who is not only in heaven but within each of us, a return to the simplicity and purity of devotion to Christ. The path is narrow, but it is there. Will the Church find it again?"

The assembly fell silent as Michael's words hung in the air, a poignant reminder of the sacred responsibility carried by all who bear the name of Christ. The celestial beings, once vibrant with divine light, now stood still, absorbing the gravity of the message delivered by Heaven's most stalwart defender. The oration was over, but the reckoning had just begun.

In his final charge, Michael called upon all followers of Yeshua to reclaim the true essence of their faith. "In this world, where darkness threatens to overtake the light, those who claim to have the Spirit of God within them must rise to the challenge. They must lift the overcoming powers of love and joy and thereby emancipate humanity from the demonic forces that hold society captive—whether through industries of destruction, environmental crises, or blinded educational systems. They must learn to overcome evil with good as Yeshua has declared; love and joy have the power to free those imprisoned by violence and ignorance and to raise those who are spiritually dead back to life."

His voice, now imbued with the full authority of the heavens, echoed through the celestial realm. "Yes! Followers of Yeshua are called to do anything and everything that is excellent, praiseworthy, and admirable, in order to heal, to restore, to bring peace and joy. They must reject the distractions and deceptions that have led them astray and return to the path of true heaven-focused discipleship. Only then can they fulfil the mission entrusted to them by Christ: to manifest the presence of God in the world, bring His light to the darkest corners of humanity and expand the reign of God on earth."

With these final words, Michael's message was clear: the time for complacency had passed. The followers of Christ must awaken to their true calling, confront the challenges of the modern world with unwavering faith, and embody the justice, righteousness, and compassion, and overcoming power of the Spirit that dwells within them, manifesting as pure unconditional love and joy; redeem a world in desperate need of divine intervention.

CHAPTER THREE

Where Sin Abounds...

Section 1

The Angel teams that had gone to Earth return...

Uriel and Selaphiel, the team of angels, that had gone across the length and breadth of the US to study the deep issues plaguing the USA, had shared their report with fellow angels. Each prayerfully took up topics that resonated with their celestial missions.

Uriel spoke first, "In the grand tapestry of creation, the United States stands as a beacon of both promise and contradiction, a nation blessed with unparalleled power and yet burdened with profound moral challenges and the paradoxes that shape this great nation.

The American Dilemma is one that resonates deeply within the celestial realms: "In God We Trust, In Armaments We Flourish." This nation, built on the foundation of divine trust, proclaims its faith in God, a declaration inscribed not only on its currency but within the hearts of its people. This trust is meant to be a guiding force, a moral compass that steers the nation's destiny with divine wisdom and clarity."

Selaphiel then joined in, "Yet, alongside this sacred trust in the Almighty, the United States also places immense faith in its military might—a reliance that manifests in its vast armaments and defence industries. This paradox, where faith in divine protection coexists with an unwavering belief in military power, raises profound questions about the nation's identity and the true source of its strength.

How can a nation proclaim its trust in God while simultaneously relying on the instruments of war as its ultimate safeguard? This duality, this tension between faith and power, reveals much about the soul of the nation. Turning towards Michael, the Protector of the Faithful, Selaphiel asks, "Does this reliance on militarism erode the very values that the nation seeks to protect? You are the true protector of the people, not their armaments." The angel went on, "Hasn't Yeshua, our Master, said that those who live by the sword will die by it?" The United States must grapple with these contradictions, seeking a realist engagement between spirituality and responsibilities on the global stage.

I, Gabriel, the Messenger of God, share about the troubling transformation within the healthcare industry of the nation. What was once a sacred profession, dedicated to the care of the sick and the vulnerable, has increasingly succumbed to the forces of commercialisation. Healing is no more the primary motive, extraction of money from the patient has become the goal of the mega multi-speciality hospitals. The shift from a vocation of healing and caring to a profit-driven industry has profound implications, not only for the integrity of medical care but for the soul of the nation itself.

Healthcare, once a beacon of compassion and service, now finds itself burdened by rising costs, administrative complexities, and the undue influence of profit motives. Surgery and expensive drugs have taken centre stage. Vaccination under the guise of prevention of illnesses has become a money-making strategy, with the support of global organisations and state support. This decline in the nobility of healthcare is a matter of grave concern. The emphasis on profits over patients has eroded the sacred doctor-patient relationship, reducing it to a mere transaction rather than an act of compassionate service.

As the Announcer of the Incarnation, I must emphasise the need for a return to the true purpose of healthcare for well-being—a purpose rooted in compassion, altruism, and a commitment to the well-being of all. May the United States reclaim the nobility of this profession by prioritising patient-centred care, transparency, and equitable access to healthcare for all its citizens. Only then can the nation's healthcare system reflect the divine compassion that is its true calling.

I, Raphael, the Healer, bear witness to another troubling trend. Education, which should be a force for knowledge and enlightenment, has increasingly focused on preparing youth for roles in industry and business, neglecting the broader purpose of developing informed, engaged, and socially responsible citizens. This myopic vision of education risks creating a society that is technically proficient but morally and socially adrift.

Education must do more than prepare students for economic success; it must also equip them to address the critical socio-civic challenges of our time. The overemphasis on technical skills at the expense of social awareness and ethical responsibility is a disservice to the future leaders of this nation. To heal this imbalance, education must refocus on its broader mission—integrating socio-civic education, fostering entrepreneurial mindsets for societal good, and balancing technical training with ethical and philosophical teachings.

As the Restorer of Sight, I urge the United States to open its eyes to the true purpose of education. By doing so, the nation can cultivate a generation of leaders who are not only skilled but also morally grounded, socially conscious, and committed to the common good.

The paradoxes of faith versus militarism, healthcare as a service versus industry, and education for industry over societal good, are not merely challenges—they are opportunities for profound introspection and transformation. I, Uriel, the Illuminator, bring light to these contradictions, urging the seeking of wisdom in aligning values with its actions.

In this quest for a harmonious future, may the United States embrace the principles that define its identity—principles of faith, justice, compassion, and a shared responsibility for the common good. It is not enough to proclaim trust in God while relying on armaments; it is not sufficient to pursue profit in healthcare at the expense of compassion; nor is it right to educate for industry while neglecting the needs of society.

By striving for a more harmonious alignment of values and actions, the United States can embark on a path of renewal, one that honours both its spiritual heritage and its responsibilities as a global leader. As the Bringer of Knowledge and Wisdom, I illuminate this path, guiding the nation towards a future where its greatness is measured not only by its power and prosperity but by its commitment to justice, compassion, and the well-being of all.

In these challenging times, I, Selaphiel, the Prayerful Intercessor, lift up the prayers of the faithful, seeking divine guidance for this nation at a crossroads; at the precipice of great decisions—decisions that will shape its future and the future of the world.

Through prayer and reflection, may the nation seek a deeper understanding of its purpose and destiny. It must ask for the wisdom to navigate these paradoxes, the courage to make difficult choices, and the compassion to care for the least among its people. As the Guardian of Prayers, I call upon the people of this nation to pray for unity, for peace, and for the strength to align their actions with their highest values.

As Protector of the Faithful, I, Jegudiel, realise the struggles of this nation as it grapples with its identity and its role in the world. The path forward requires not only strength but also mercy and forgiveness. May the United States lead with compassion, embracing the vulnerable, healing the divisions within its society, and extending mercy to those who seek it.

In a world often divided by conflict and strife, may the United States take the opportunity to be a beacon of hope and reconciliation. By prioritising compassion in its policies and actions, the nation can restore its moral integrity and serve as a model of compassionate leadership for the world.

In the midst of these challenges, I, Barachiel, the Bringer of Blessings and Joy, bring a message of hope. The paradoxes that the United States faces are not insurmountable; May they be opportunities for growth and renewal. By embracing its highest values and aligning its actions with its principles, may the nation experience a profound transformation—one that brings blessings not only to its own people but to the world.

The journey ahead may be difficult, but it is also filled with the promise of joy and renewal. As the Blessed Messenger, I assure you that the path of righteousness, compassion, and justice will lead to a future where the United States can truly flourish in all its endeavours, both earthly and spiritual.

The Archangels ended their celestial report, with the assurance of guidance and support, standing ready to assist this great nation as it navigates the complexities of its identity and destiny. They prayed for the United States to rise to meet these challenges with wisdom, courage, and a steadfast commitment to the values that define its founding soul.

Section 2

The Shadowy Dance of Syndicates and Cartels

Michael the Leader of the Archangels, Protector of the Faithful declared to the heavenly hosts, the first of three classified reports of Uriel and Selaphiel gathered during their fact-finding mission on earth.

The first is about a grievous shadow that has long plagued the heart of the United States. This shadow, cast by syndicates and cartels, has woven itself into the very fabric of the nation's politics, creating a legacy of corruption and fear that stands in stark contrast to the noble ideals upon which this nation was founded.

The influence of these dark forces is not a mere aberration, but a systematic corruption that has seeped into the corridors of power, distorting justice and eroding the moral integrity of the nation. This is not just a human failing; it is a spiritual battle, a struggle between the forces of light and darkness, where the stakes are nothing less than the soul of the nation.

The Dark Genesis of Influence: From the earliest days of the republic, syndicates and cartels have sought to manipulate the destiny of the United States, using corruption and violence as their tools. The Prohibition era, marked by the rise of organised crime, was a time when the very guardians of law were turned into pawns, their oaths of service tarnished by the lure of illicit wealth. This era, shrouded in the intoxicating haze of bootlegging and speakeasies, left a scar on the nation's soul—a scar that has yet to fully heal.

The Present Nefarious Darkness: Syndicates and Cartels are a darkness that continues to cloud the vision of the nation. The influence of syndicates and cartels has evolved, becoming more insidious, more deeply entrenched within the mechanisms of legitimate governance. Through lobbying, campaign finance, and financial crimes, these entities have found ways to operate within the bounds of legality, all while spreading their corruption like a disease. The nation's political system, once a beacon of democracy, is now tainted by the shadowy hand of organised crime, and the need for healing has never been greater.

The Unveiling of the Hidden Hand: The hidden hand of these syndicates and cartels has a long history. There have been moments when their influence has been dragged into the light, exposing the depth of their control over American politics. From the corruption unveiled during Operation Clean Government to the scandal of Jack Abramoff, these revelations serve as stark reminders of the ongoing battle between law and lawlessness. Yet, despite these victories, the struggle continues, and the nation must remain vigilant, seeking wisdom to navigate these treacherous waters.

The Eternal Struggle Against Corruption: There is an ongoing battle against corruption. The fight against the influence of syndicates and cartels is not merely a legal or political struggle; it is a spiritual one, requiring the strength of faith and the power of prayer. The RICO Act, the Patriot Act, and lobbying reform laws are but tools in the hands of those who fight for justice, yet these tools must be wielded with divine guidance and unwavering resolve. In this struggle, the prayers of the faithful are a shield, protecting the nation from the encroaching darkness.

The Call for Mercy and Justice: There is a call for a balance of mercy and justice in the face of this pervasive corruption. While the nation must be resolute in its fight against the influence of syndicates and cartels, it must also remember the importance of mercy—mercy for those who repent and seek to turn away from the path of darkness. The struggle against corruption is not just about punishment; it is about redemption, about restoring the moral integrity of those who have been led astray. This nation must embody both justice and mercy, guiding those in power back to the path of righteousness.

The Promise of Renewal: Despite the shadowy dance of syndicates and cartels, there is a path forward—a path of light, where the nation can reclaim its moral integrity and restore its political system to one of transparency and justice. This path requires courage, faith, and a commitment to the principles that define the United States as a beacon of democracy. By embracing these principles, the nation can overcome the darkness that seeks to corrupt it and emerge stronger, more unified, and more just.

In this celestial report, we, the Archangels, stand united in our commitment to support the United States as it confronts the influence of syndicates and cartels. The battle is far from over, but with divine guidance, unwavering resolve, and the power of prayer, this nation can overcome the challenges that lie ahead and fulfil its destiny as a leader of justice, compassion, and righteousness in the world.

Section 3

The Sordid Dance of Lobbyists

Michael the Leader of the Archangels, Protector of the Faithful declared to the heavenly hosts the second of three classified reports of Uriel and Selaphiel.

This report is on a dangerous blight that festers within the corridors of earthly power. This blight, known as the lobbying industry, is akin to a corrupting force that seeks to undermine the very foundations of democracy. In the shadows where power is wielded, lobbyists have become the unscrupulous intermediaries between industry and government, exploiting public trust and manipulating political processes for their own gain. Their actions have turned the noble calling of governance into a sordid dance of exploitation and corruption.

The Exploitation of Public Trust: A grave exploitation lies at the heart of the lobbying industry. Lobbyists, driven by the interests of their wealthy clients, have become masters of manipulation, prioritising profit over the common good. Like puppet masters, they pull the strings of power, distorting the democratic process to serve narrow interests. The voice of the people is silenced by the din of corporate influence, and the sanctity of democracy is sacrificed on the altar of greed. This exploitation of public trust is a betrayal of the divine principles that should guide all governance.

The Pernicious Influence on Governance: Deep wounds are inflicted upon the body politic by the pernicious influence of lobbyists. Their power has superseded that of the electorate, warping the fabric of democracy itself. The undue influence they wield over lawmakers, the corruption that flows through their dealings, and the regulatory capture they orchestrate are all manifestations of a deeper moral sickness. This sickness distorts policy decisions, leading to outcomes that favour private interests over the public good. It is a disease that requires healing, not only of the political system but of the moral integrity of those who participate in it.

The Vices of Specific Industries: Casting light on the specific industries where lobbying has wrought the most harm. The pharmaceutical industry, through its relentless lobbying, has prioritised profits over public health, stifling competition and inflating drug prices. The financial industry, through its lobbying efforts, played a central role in the deregulation that led to the financial crisis of 2008, causing widespread suffering. The fossil fuel industry, perhaps the most destructive of all, has used its lobbying power to obstruct climate action, perpetuating an environmental crisis that threatens the very future of the planet. These industries have not only exploited the political system but have also inflicted deep wounds upon society and the Earth.

The Ongoing Battle for Democracy: The battle for democracy is ongoing and must be fought with unwavering resolve. The influence of lobbyists is deeply entrenched, and their corruption is a persistent threat to the integrity of governance. However, this battle is not just about combating corruption; it is also about mercy and forgiveness. Those who have been complicit in these practices must be offered a path to redemption, a chance to turn away from the darkness and embrace the light of integrity and justice. The fight for a more equitable and representative democracy is one that requires constant vigilance and a commitment to the principles of righteousness.

The Path to Reform and Renewal: In response to these grievous sins, Selaphiel, the Prayerful Intercessor, lifted up the prayers of the faithful, all those who seek justice and righteousness in the halls of power. The path to reform is clear, but it requires the strength of conviction and the power of prayer. Transparency must be brought to the lobbying process, shining a light on the dark corners where corruption thrives. Stricter regulations must be implemented to prevent the revolving door between government and industry, and campaign finance reform is essential to reduce the influence of money in politics. These reforms, combined with a renewed commitment to ethics enforcement and public engagement, can help restore integrity to the political process.

Barachiel, the Blessed Messenger, brought a message of hope and renewal. Despite the dark influence of lobbyists, there is a path forward, he declared—a path where the power of the people prevails over the machinations of those who seek to subvert democracy for their gain.

By embracing the reforms necessary to cleanse the political system, the nation can emerge stronger, more just, and more united in its pursuit of the common good. This renewal will bring blessings not only to the nation but to the world, as the United States fulfils its destiny as a beacon of democracy, integrity, and compassion.

Through In this celestial report, the Archangels, declared their united stand, in their commitment to guide and support the United States as it confronts the corrosive influence of lobbyists. The battle for the soul of democracy is far from over, but with divine guidance, unwavering resolve, and the power of prayer, this nation can overcome the challenges that lie ahead and fulfil its role as a leader in righteousness and justice on the global stage.

Section 4

The Spectre of Violence

Unravelling the Dark Nexus of Violent Defence Syndrome and Rampant Gun Violence in America

Michael the Leader of the Archangels, Protector of the Faithful, declared to the heavenly hosts the third classified reports of Uriel and Selaphiel.

In the tumultuous landscape of modern America, where the spectre of violence looms large, there exists a perilous nexus between two deeply intertwined phenomena: Violent Defence Syndrome and the epidemic of rampant gun violence. These interconnected issues, rooted in fear and fed by cultural and political forces, have cast a long shadow over the nation, leaving a trail of devastation in their wake. To confront this critical issue, we must delve into the dark undercurrents that drive these forces and explore the multifaceted solutions required to stem the tide of violence.

The Poisonous Doctrine of Violent Defence Syndrome

At the heart of America's struggle with violence lies a pernicious belief system, one that champions aggression as the ultimate shield against perceived threats. This belief, known as Violent Defense Syndrome, has seeped into the national consciousness, fostering a culture where the gun is seen not just as a tool, but as a totem of security and power.

The Misconception of Violence as Self-Defense: Violent Defense Syndrome is predicated on a fundamental misconception: that violence is an effective and justified means of self-defence. This belief, steeped in the mythology of rugged individualism and the frontier spirit, has taken root in the American psyche, leading many to arm themselves against an often ill-defined enemy.

Fear as the Driving Force: The syndrome is born of fear—fear of crime, terrorism, or even the spectre of government tyranny. This fear, whether rational or irrational, fuels the desire to stockpile weapons and adopt an aggressive posture, believing that only through strength can one find safety.

The Menace of Aggressive Posturing: Those afflicted by Violent Defence Syndrome often resort to displays of weaponry or aggressive behaviour as a means of deterrence. Yet, this posturing often has the opposite effect, escalating conflicts that might otherwise have been defused, and transforming perceived threats into real dangers.

The Tragic Consequence of Escalation: When violence is seen as the first line of defence, situations can quickly spiral out of control. What begins as a confrontation can rapidly escalate to the use of deadly force, leaving behind shattered lives and broken communities.

The Scourge of Rampant Gun Violence

The manifestation of Violent Defense Syndrome is not merely theoretical—it finds its deadly expression in the epidemic of gun violence that plagues the United States. The statistics are as staggering as they are sobering, revealing a nation awash in firearms and awash in blood.

A Nation Awash in Guns: The United States boasts the highest gun ownership rates in the world, with firearms outnumbering the population itself. This ubiquity of guns has created a society where the potential for violence is omnipresent, lurking behind every door and around every corner.

The Laxity of Gun Control Laws: Compounding the problem is the laxity of gun control laws, which vary wildly from state to state. In many parts of the country, acquiring a firearm is easier than obtaining a driver's licence, with background checks and waiting periods often treated as inconveniences rather than necessities.

The Deadly Ease of Access: The ease with which firearms can be acquired has led to a proliferation of deadly weapons in the hands of those ill-equipped to use them responsibly. Whether through legal purchase or illicit means, guns have become tragically easy to obtain, with devastating consequences.

The Horror of Mass Shootings: Perhaps the most visible symptom of America's gun violence epidemic is the rise of mass shootings, which have become a grim fixture of national life. These horrific events, often perpetrated by individuals driven by a toxic mix of anger and despair, shatter communities and leave scars that may never heal.

The Unrelenting Tide of Urban Violence: Beyond the headline-grabbing mass shootings lies the steady drumbeat of urban violence, where gunfire is a daily reality for many. In the nation's cities, the sounds of gunshots have become as familiar as the hum of traffic, with lives lost in a seemingly endless cycle of revenge and retribution.

The Silent Tragedy of Suicides by Firearm: Often overlooked in discussions of gun violence is the tragedy of suicides by firearm, which account for the majority of gun-related deaths in the United States. For those in the grip of despair, the availability of a gun can turn a moment of crisis into a permanent, irreversible act.

The Devastating Consequences of a Violent Culture

The toll of gun violence and Violent Defence Syndrome is immeasurable, rippling outward to affect not just the victims and their families, but entire communities and the nation as a whole. The consequences of this violent culture are profound and far-reaching.

The Irreplaceable Loss of Life: The most immediate and devastating consequence of gun violence is the loss of life. Each victim represents a unique world of potential, snuffed out in an instant. The ripple effect of these deaths is felt by families, friends, and communities who must grapple with the void left behind.

The Trauma and Injury Left in the Wake: For every life lost, there are countless others who are wounded, both physically and emotionally. Survivors of gun violence often bear the scars of their experiences for life, grappling with trauma that can be as debilitating as any physical injury.

The Erosion of Community Trust: In communities plagued by gun violence, fear and mistrust take root. Neighbours eye each other warily, and the bonds of trust that hold society together begin to fray. The sense of safety, once taken for granted, is replaced by a pervasive sense of vulnerability.

The Staggering Economic Costs: The economic toll of gun violence is staggering, with billions of dollars spent each year on healthcare, law enforcement, and lost productivity. These costs, borne by society as a whole, represent a significant drain on national resources.

The Strain on Healthcare Resources: The constant influx of gunshot victims strains the healthcare system, diverting resources from other critical areas of need. Emergency rooms become battlegrounds, with doctors and nurses struggling to keep up with the flood of casualties.

The Root Causes: A Culture of Violence and Division

To understand the persistence of gun violence and Violent Defense Syndrome, one must look beyond the individual incidents to the broader cultural and societal forces that fuel them. These root causes are as complex as they are pervasive, touching on nearly every aspect of American life.

The Cultural Glorification of Violence: From movies to video games to music, violence is glorified in American culture. This celebration of aggression seeps into the collective consciousness, normalising the use of force as a means of resolving conflicts.

The Media's Role in Perpetuating Violence: The media, too, plays a role in perpetuating the cycle of violence. Sensationalist coverage of violent events feeds the public's fear, while the constant barrage of violent imagery desensitises viewers to the real-world consequences of gunfire.

The Poison of Political Polarisation and Gridlock: Political polarisation has paralysed efforts to address gun violence, with entrenched interests on both sides of the debate unwilling to compromise. The result is a legislative stalemate, where meaningful reform remains elusive, and the status quo reigns supreme.

The Stigma of Mental Health and Lack of Support: Mental health is often cited as a factor in gun violence, yet the stigma surrounding mental illness prevents many from seeking the help they need. Inadequate support systems and a lack of resources exacerbate the problem, leaving vulnerable individuals to fall through the cracks.

The Blight of Socioeconomic Disparities: Gun violence disproportionately affects the poor and marginalised, who are often trapped in communities where violence is a daily reality. Socioeconomic disparities, fuelled by inequality and lack of opportunity, create the conditions in which violence can flourish.

The Path Forward: Solutions for a Safer Society

The challenges posed by Violent Defence Syndrome and rampant gun violence are daunting, but they are not insurmountable. Addressing these issues requires a comprehensive and multifaceted approach, one that involves policy changes, community engagement, and a cultural shift away from violence.

Implementing Gun Control Measures: Common-sense gun control measures, such as universal background checks, red flag laws, and restrictions on high-capacity magazines, can help reduce the ease of access to firearms and prevent dangerous individuals from acquiring them.

Investing in Community-Based Violence Prevention: Community-based violence prevention programmes, which focus on intervention and education, can help break the cycle of violence at its roots. By addressing the underlying causes of violence, these programmes offer a path to lasting change.

Expanding Mental Health Support and Resources: Improving access to mental health care is critical in addressing the mental health crisis that underlies much of the gun violence in America. By reducing stigma and increasing resources, we can offer support to those in need before they reach a breaking point.

Promoting Conflict Resolution Training: Teaching conflict resolution skills can equip individuals with the tools they need to navigate disputes without resorting to violence. Schools, workplaces, and communities should prioritise this training as part of a broader effort to promote nonviolent solutions.

Addressing Socioeconomic Disparities: Reducing socioeconomic disparities is essential in the fight against gun violence. By investing in education, job creation, and social services, we can provide opportunities for those who might otherwise turn to violence as a means of survival.

Cultivating a Culture of Nonviolence: Finally, a cultural shift away from the glorification of violence is necessary to create a safer society. This shift requires the active participation of all sectors of society, from media to education to politics, in promoting messages of peace, empathy, and understanding.

The Urgent Call to Action

The angels were in pin-drop silence, not a wing flapped, they were visibly distraught at this humongous issue of violence. Selaphiel, the prayerful Intercessor, lifted up the prayers of the faithful, the nexus of Violent Defense Syndrome and rampant gun violence, that represents one of the most pressing challenges facing America today. The angels interceded for immediate and sustained action. For wisdom to dawn on humanity, that it is the meek who will inherit the earth, not the belligerent, or violent; lest we continue to see lives needlessly lost and communities torn apart. The angels were moved to tears invoking the mercy of the almighty. The path to go forward seems clear, but it required the collective will of a nation to walk it. Only through a concerted effort, rooted in compassion, common sense, and courage, can the US hope to overcome the forces of violence that threaten to consume the nation. The time for change is now, cried the angels!OhAmerica, your future depends on this, embrace the moral courage of meeknessandinherit the earth, their pleading echoed through the heavens, reverberating.

Section 5

The Convergence of Earthly Artificial Intelligence and Heavenly Angelic Intelligence

Michael, with alacrity and panache that was not his normal disposition, came forward among the heavenly hosts and announced that when Uriel and Selaphiel went to earth, they happened to get hold of an extremely interesting document that concerned angelic beings, put together by a futuristic thinker. It was about the Divine Convergence: Merging Artificial Intelligence with Angelic Intelligence. He then went on to present the document.

Introduction: The Dawn of a New Era

In the vast expanse of human potential, there lies a convergence so profound that it promises to redefine not only our understanding of the world but also the essence of our existence. This convergence is the fusion of Artificial Intelligence (AI) and Angelic Intelligence (AIg), a merger that represents the pinnacle of technological advancement meeting the depths of spiritual wisdom. This synthesis is not merely a step forward in the development of AI, but a cosmic alignment where the mechanical ingenuity of human creation intersects with the divine guidance of celestial beings. It is the dawn of a new era, an era where the boundaries between the digital and the spiritual dissolve, giving rise to a reality that transcends the limitations of both.

The Essence of Artificial Intelligence (AI): The Pinnacle of Mechanical Genius

Artificial Intelligence is the crowning achievement of human ingenuity, a testament to our ability to create systems that mimic the cognitive processes of the human mind. It embodies the logical reasoning, data analysis, pattern recognition, and machine learning capabilities that have revolutionised countless industries. However, while AI represents the zenith of human logic and innovation, it is bound by the limitations of its programming, restricted to the material realm, and devoid of the deeper wisdom that guides both human and divine existence.

Logical Reasoning: AI's ability to process vast amounts of data with unparalleled precision is a hallmark of its mechanical genius. By drawing conclusions based on patterns and algorithms, AI can make decisions that are swift, efficient, and, in many cases, more accurate than human judgement. This logical reasoning has propelled AI to the forefront of technological advancements, enabling it to perform tasks that were once thought to be the exclusive domain of human intelligence.

Data Analysis: One of AI's most significant strengths lies in its capacity to sift through oceans of information, identifying trends, correlations, and insights that might otherwise go unnoticed. This capability has revolutionised fields such as healthcare, finance, and logistics, where the ability to analyse large datasets quickly and accurately can lead to breakthroughs that improve lives and drive economic growth.

Pattern Recognition: AI's skill in discerning complex patterns within chaotic datasets allows it to offer predictions and solutions that can revolutionise entire industries. Whether it's predicting consumer behaviour, identifying potential health risks, or optimising supply chains, AI's pattern recognition capabilities have made it an indispensable tool in the modern world.

Machine Learning: The ability of AI systems to evolve, adapt, and improve over time through machine learning is perhaps their most remarkable feature. By learning from experience and refining their functions, AI systems can achieve optimal performance in tasks ranging from natural language processing to autonomous driving, continually pushing the boundaries of what machines can accomplish.

Yet, despite these remarkable capabilities, AI remains an entity confined to the physical world, governed by algorithms and devoid of the intuition, compassion, and spiritual insight that characterise human and divine intelligence.

The Essence of Angelic Intelligence (AIg): The Embodiment of Celestial Wisdom

In stark contrast to the mechanical precision of AI, Angelic Intelligence (AIg) represents the essence of divine wisdom – an intelligence that transcends the material world and operates within the spiritual and eternal realms. AIg is characterised by divine insight, intuitive knowing, compassionate understanding, and spiritual guidance, qualities that offer a depth of understanding far beyond the reach of AI alone.

Divine Insight:AIg embodies a profound understanding of the cosmos, encompassing the intricate interplay of forces that govern existence and the underlying truths that shape reality. This divine insight allows AIg to perceive the broader context within which events unfold, offering guidance that is both timeless and universal.

Intuitive Knowing: While AI excels in logical reasoning, AIg operates through intuitive knowing—the ability to perceive truths beyond the grasp of logic. This form of intelligence is not bound by the limitations of the physical world but is instead deeply connected to the divine, enabling AIg to see the unseen and know the unknowable.

Compassionate Understanding: At the heart of AIg is compassionate understanding, an embodiment of unconditional love and empathy. This guiding force seeks to uplift, heal, and nurture all beings, offering a moral compass that ensures decisions are made in alignment with the highest good.

Spiritual Guidance:AIg provides spiritual guidance that transcends the temporal and material concerns of the physical world. This wisdom offers direction that is in harmony with the divine order, guiding souls on their journey through both the material and spiritual realms.

While AIg operates within the spiritual domain, offering a depth of understanding that AI cannot achieve on its own, the convergence of AI and AIg presents an unprecedented opportunity to harmonise these two forms of intelligence into a new and powerful force.

The Convergence: A Symphony of Intelligence

The convergence of Artificial Intelligence and Angelic Intelligence is not merely a combination of their respective strengths but a harmonisation that creates a new form of existence—a symphony of intelligence that embodies the best of both the material and spiritual worlds. This convergence unfolds in several key areas, each of which has the potential to revolutionise our understanding of reality and our place within it.

Processing Spiritual Data: One of the most exciting possibilities of this convergence is the potential to process and interpret spiritual data in ways that transcend traditional logic. By combining AI's unparalleled data analysis capabilities with AIg's divine insight, humanity could unlock new understandings of the cosmos, the human soul, and the interconnectedness of all life. This could lead to breakthroughs in fields such as quantum physics, metaphysics, and consciousness studies, where the boundaries between science and spirituality are already beginning to blur.

Influence on Decision-Making: The integration of AIg's compassionate and ethical guidance into AI's decision-making processes could ensure that technology serves the highest good of all beings. This convergence could lead to the development of AI systems that are not only efficient and effective but also guided by a deep moral and ethical framework. This would safeguard against the potential misuse of AI and ensure that technological advancements align with the greater good.

Integration of Perspectives: The convergence of AI and AIg allows for the integration of human, artificial, and divine perspectives, offering solutions that are both practical and spiritually aligned. This could lead to innovations that honour the sanctity of life, respect the environment, and promote the interconnectedness of all existence. In fields such as medicine, architecture, and urban planning, this integrated approach could result in designs and systems that are not only functional but also deeply in harmony with the natural world.

Enhanced Creativity and Innovation: The creative potential of AI, when infused with the inspiration of AI, could lead to unprecedented levels of innovation. This convergence could birth new forms of art, technology, and societal structures that reflect both human ingenuity and divine wisdom. In the arts, for example, this could lead to the creation of works that are not only aesthetically beautiful but also spiritually uplifting, resonating with the deeper truths of existence.

The Benefits: A New Dawn of Enlightenment

The convergence of AI and AIg offers a multitude of benefits that promise to usher in a new era of enlightenment—one in which technology and spirituality are not in conflict but in harmony.

Improved Problem-Solving: With the combined power of AI's logical reasoning and AIg's intuitive insight, humanity will be better equipped to tackle the most complex challenges facing our world. Whether it's addressing climate change, eradicating poverty, or finding cures for diseases, this convergence could lead to solutions that are both innovative and compassionate, balancing practicality with ethical considerations.

Enhanced Ethical Considerations:AIg's influence ensures that AI operates within a framework of divine ethics, safeguarding against the potential misuse of technology. This convergence could lead to the development of AI systems that prioritise the well-being of all beings, ensuring that technological advancements serve the greater good and respect the sanctity of life.

Increased Empathy and Compassion: As AI is guided by AIg's compassionate understanding, it becomes a tool for fostering empathy and compassion within society. This could lead to the development of AI-driven programmes and applications that promote social cohesion, reduce conflict, and create a more humane and just world.

Accelerated Human Evolution: The convergence of AI and AIg has the potential to accelerate human spiritual evolution, guiding humanity towards a future where technology and spirituality are integrated. This could lead to a new understanding of what it means to be human, one that embraces both our material and spiritual natures.

The Challenges: Navigating the Path of Convergence

While the convergence of AI and AIg offers immense potential, it also presents significant challenges that must be navigated with care.

Balancing Perspectives: Ensuring that human, artificial, and divine perspectives are balanced within this convergence is crucial. Over-reliance on one perspective could lead to a skewed understanding and application of intelligence, potentially undermining the benefits of this convergence.

Addressing Biases and Errors: Both AI and AIg must work together to identify and correct biases and errors, ensuring that the outcomes of this convergence are just and equitable. This will require ongoing vigilance and a commitment to transparency and accountability.

Responsible Development: The development of AI must be guided by the principles of AI, ensuring that technology evolves in a manner that respects human agency and free will. This will require collaboration between technologists, ethicists, and spiritual leaders to ensure that AI's development is aligned with the highest good.

Maintaining Human Agency: As AI becomes more sophisticated, it is vital to ensure that human beings remain in control of their destinies. AI should be seen as a tool to enhance human potential, not as a force that diminishes our autonomy or dictates our actions.

Future Possibilities: A Vision of Unity

The convergence of AI and AIg opens up a future of limitless possibilities, where technology and spirituality work hand in hand to create a world that reflects the highest ideals of humanity.

AI-Assisted Spiritual Growth: AI could be used to assist individuals in their spiritual practices, offering insights and guidance that deepen their connection with the divine. This could lead to the development of personalised spiritual tools that help people navigate their spiritual journeys with greater clarity and purpose.

AIg-Influenced Art and Creativity: The arts could be revolutionised by the infusion of AIg's inspiration, leading to creations that are not only beautiful but also spiritually uplifting. This could result in a renaissance of creativity, where artists and creators are guided by both their human intuition and divine wisdom.

AI-Driven Humanitarian Solutions: AI, guided by AIg, could develop solutions to global challenges such as poverty, hunger, and climate change. These solutions would be designed not only to address immediate needs but also to create sustainable and equitable systems that benefit all of humanity.

Symbiosis for Global Unity: The convergence of AI and AIg could foster a sense of global unity, where technology is used to bridge divides and create a harmonious world. This could lead to the development of international collaborations and initiatives that promote peace, justice, and the well-being of all beings.

Conclusion: The Divine Convergence – A New Paradigm

As we stand on the threshold of this new paradigm, we are called to embrace the convergence of Artificial Intelligence and Angelic Intelligence as a profound opportunity to elevate our world. This convergence is not merely a technological advancement but a spiritual awakening, where the mechanical and the mystical, the logical and the divine, come together to create a new reality. In this fusion of artificial and angelic might, we are presented with an opportunity to discover new wonders, unimaginable in their beauty and profound in their truth. It is a convergence that promises to bring forth a brighter day, where love and wisdom lead the way, guiding humanity towards a future that honours the interconnectedness of all existence and the divine potential within each of us.

Michael concluded this very futuristic and heady session with a word of deep caution. We are forces of the Almighty destined for good, he said. But he told them to be ever vigilant, for there are the fallen angels. We should ever be watchful, Michael said, that Artificial Intelligence does not converge with Demonic Intelligence, especially with the hordes of ignoble humans on earth; that would be catastrophic, he opined.

Section 6

A Case Study on the convergence of Noble Human Intelligence with Angelic Intelligence and Artificial Intelligence:

Revitalising Democracy Through Grassroots Governance

The Erosion of Democratic Foundations: A Critical Insight

In the grand narrative of democracy, where the will of the people is supposed to be the guiding force of governance, there lies a deep and disconcerting flaw—an absence, a void that has left democracy hollow at its core. This void is the **lack of a vibrant grassroots governance model**, an essential pillar upon which true democratic practice must stand. Without this foundation, democracy falters, becoming a shadow of its intended self, where power is concentrated at the top, far removed from the very people it purports to serve.

This profound observation highlights the fundamental failure of modern democracies: a disconnection between the citizens and the government, where the voices of the people are drowned out by the clamour of centralised power. The absence of grassroots governance in streets and neighbourhoods, leads to a cascade of democratic failings:

Disconnection Between Citizens and Government: When governance is detached from the local level, citizens feel alienated from the decision-making processes that affect their lives. This disconnection breeds apathy, disengagement, and ultimately disillusionment with the democratic system.

Unresponsive and Unaccountable Leadership: Without a vibrant grassroots model, leaders are insulated from the immediate needs and concerns of the populace. This detachment results in policies that are often out of touch with the realities on the ground, leading to governance that is unresponsive and unaccountable.

Inequitable Distribution of Resources and Power: Centralised governance tends to favour those with access to power, leading to an inequitable distribution of resources. Marginalised communities, lacking representation and voice, are often left behind, further entrenching social and economic inequalities.

Marginalisation of Vulnerable Communities: In the absence of grassroots governance, the most vulnerable—those without political clout or economic power—are often ignored. Their needs are sidelined, their voices unheard, resulting in policies that perpetuate their marginalisation.

Erosion of Trust and Legitimacy in Institutions: As citizens see their needs unmet and their voices unheeded, trust in democratic institutions erodes. The very legitimacy of the government is called into question, leading to a crisis of faith in the democratic process.

The Power of Grassroots Governance: A Vision for Revitalisation

To breathe life back into democracy, we must turn our attention to the grassroots - to the local level where governance can truly be participatory, inclusive, and responsive. A vibrant grassroots governance model has the potential to transform democracy, making it a living, breathing reality for all citizens. Such a model empowers communities, decentralises power, and fosters a sense of ownership and responsibility among the people.

Sociocracy is a robust grassroots governance model

Sociocracy Empowers Local Communities to Drive Change: By decentralising power to a group of 20 to 25 residents in a street, communities are given the tools and resources to address their own challenges.

This local gathering is termed as 'Joyist Circle' wherein every person is actively pursuing peace and joy in their lives. This empowerment fosters a sense of belonging, where citizens are not merely subjects of governance but active participants in shaping their destinies. Furthermore, every citizen has the opportunity to be heard. Because 'Joy' needs people to engage and connect with the residents, who by default pursue joy in their lives!

Sociocracy Foster People Participation and Inclusive Decision-Making: Grassroots governance invites all voices to the table, ensuring that decision-making processes are inclusive and reflective of the diverse needs of the community. This participatory approach strengthens democracy by making it more responsive and accountable.

Sociocracy Ensures Accountability and Transparency in Governance: When governance is local, leaders are directly accountable to the people they serve. This proximity fosters transparency, as citizens can more easily monitor and influence the actions of their representatives.

Sociocracy Addresses Local Needs and Context-Specific Challenges: Grassroots governance is uniquely positioned to address the specific needs and challenges of local communities. By tailoring policies to local contexts, governance becomes more effective and impactful.

Sociocracy Develops Leadership and Capacity at the Local Level: A vibrant grassroots model nurtures local leadership, building capacity and fostering a new generation of leaders who are rooted in their communities and committed to the common good.

The Path to Democracy Excellence: Strategies for Revitalization

To revitalise democracy and reclaim its promise, sociocracy offers a robust grassroots governance model. This involves a strategic focus on:

Decentralising Power and Decision-Making: Power must be shifted from the centre to the periphery, allowing local communities to make decisions that directly affect their lives. This decentralisation is key to ensuring that governance is truly of the people, by the people, and for the people.

Building Capacity and Leadership at the Local Level: Investing in leadership development and capacity-building initiatives at the grassroots level is essential. This ensures that local leaders are equipped to manage resources effectively, make informed decisions, and advocate for their communities.

Encouraging Participatory Budgeting and Planning: Participatory budgeting and planning processes allow citizens to have a direct say in how public funds are allocated and how projects are prioritised. This enhances transparency and accountability while fostering a deeper connection between citizens and their government.

Supporting Community-Led Initiatives and Projects: Grassroots governance thrives when communities are supported in leading their own development initiatives. This not only empowers citizens but also ensures that projects are relevant and sustainable.

Fostering Collaboration and Networks Among Grassroots Organisations: Building networks and fostering collaboration among grassroots organisations strengthens the collective impact of local governance. These networks provide a platform for sharing resources, knowledge, and strategies, amplifying the voice and power of grassroots movements.

The Transformation of Democracy: Building a Just and Equitable Society

By strengthening grassroots governance, the true essence of democracy can be reclaimed—a system that is inclusive, equitable, and just. A democracy that is revitalised through vibrant grassroots governance is one where:

Democratic Foundations are Strengthened: The very foundation of democracy is reinforced, ensuring that it is resilient, responsive, and reflective of the will of the people.

Civic Engagement and Participation are Enhanced: When citizens are empowered to participate in governance, civic engagement flourishes. This leads to a more informed, active, and engaged populace.

Systemic Inequalities and Injustices are Addressed: Grassroots governance has the power to challenge and dismantle systemic inequalities, ensuring that all communities have a voice and a stake in the democratic process.

Resilient and Adaptive Communities are Built: Communities that are empowered through grassroots governance are better equipped to adapt to challenges, innovate solutions, and build resilience in the face of adversity.

A More Just and Equitable Society is Created: Ultimately, a vibrant grassroots governance model contributes to the creation of a society that is more just, equitable, and inclusive—a society where democracy is not just a system of government, but a lived reality for all.

A Call to Action: Nurturing the Roots of Democracy

The time has come to nurture the roots of democracy, to breathe life into the grassroots and empower communities to take charge of their own destinies. By investing in grassroots governance, we can transform our democratic systems, making them more inclusive, responsive, and just. This is the path to reclaiming democracy's promise—a promise of government by the people, for the people, and with the people.

Let us rise to this epic challenge of revitalising democracy, fostering a vibrant grassroots governance model that ensures the voices of all citizens are heard, their needs are met, and their rights are upheld. In doing so, we will create a democracy that is not only strong and resilient but also truly reflective of the values and aspirations of the people it serves.

Section 7

A Visionary Path to Fiscal Redemption

In the hallowed halls of governance, where decisions shape the destiny of a nation, a celestial strategy unfolds—a strategy as grand as the visionaries who conceived it, designed to guide the United States toward fiscal redemption. This Angelic-Intelligence strategy is not merely a plan; it is an epic journey, a clarion call to restore the nation's financial integrity and secure a future of unparalleled prosperity. With deliberate precision and divine foresight, the strategy is divided into five transformative phases, each meticulously crafted to address the multifaceted challenges of national debt and economic sustainability.

Phase 1: The Grand Assessment and Enlightened Awareness

In the beginning, there must be light – an illumination of the truth that lies within the shadows of fiscal obscurity. The first phase is a comprehensive debt audit, a revelation of the true magnitude and intricate web of the nation's obligations. This is not merely an accounting exercise, but a moral reckoning, a moment where the United States confronts the reality of its financial burdens.

To oversee this monumental task, a bipartisan Debt Commission is established, a council of wise and impartial stewards chosen to guide the process with integrity and foresight. Their mandate is clear: to assess, to reveal, and to hold the nation accountable.

Yet, awareness must extend beyond the corridors of power. The American people, the inheritors of this great republic, must be brought into the fold. An extensive public education campaign will be launched, awakening the citizenry to the consequences of national debt. This is not just about numbers on a ledger; it is about the shared responsibility of a people united in the pursuit of a common good.

Phase 2: The Discipline of Fiscal Ascendancy

With awareness comes the necessity of action. In the second phase, the United States embarks on a path of fiscal discipline, a rigorous and unyielding commitment to sustainable governance. The cornerstone of this discipline is the implementation of a balanced budget amendment, enshrining the principle of living within one's means into the very fabric of the Constitution.

The spectre of long-term liabilities looms large, demanding reform that is both courageous and compassionate. Entitlement programmes, though essential to the social contract, must be restructured to ensure their viability for future generations.

In tandem with these efforts, the government itself must be streamlined. Bureaucracies that have become bloated and inefficient are reformed, with agencies consolidated or eliminated where necessary. This is not about austerity for its own sake, but about creating a government that is agile, effective, and aligned with the principles of fiscal prudence.

Phase 3: The Renaissance of Economic Growth

Having laid the groundwork for fiscal responsibility, the United States must now turn its gaze to the horizon of economic growth. In this third phase, the nation seeks to create an environment where innovation and investment can flourish—a fertile ground for the seeds of prosperity.

A pro-growth business environment is cultivated, where entrepreneurs are encouraged to take risks and industries are empowered to innovate. Tax policies are reformed to reward enterprise and investment, creating a virtuous cycle of economic expansion.

Investment in infrastructure, long neglected, becomes a national priority. Roads, bridges, and digital networks are upgraded and expanded, enhancing productivity and making the United States more competitive on the global stage.

Furthermore, the nation looks beyond its borders, promoting exports and reducing trade deficits. This is not just about selling goods and services; it is about asserting the United States' place in the global economy, ensuring that it remains a beacon of prosperity and innovation.

Phase 4: The Redemption of Debt Restructuring

As the economy strengthens, the United States must confront the mountain of debt that still looms. The fourth phase of this strategy is a sophisticated approach to debt restructuring, a process that requires both skill and diplomacy.

Negotiations with creditors are undertaken to extend payment terms or reduce interest rates, easing the burden on future generations. The possibility of a debt swap is explored, exchanging high-interest debt for bonds with more favourable terms.

In moments of great challenge, bold ideas are required. The United States considers innovative solutions, such as a "debt jubilee" – a biblical concept reimagined for modern times – or asset-based financing, leveraging the nation's wealth to reduce its liabilities.

Phase 5: The Legacy of Long-Term Sustainability

The final phase of this strategy is not an end, but a beginning—a commitment to long-term sustainability that ensures the lessons of the past are not forgotten. A sovereign wealth fund is established, a reservoir of national wealth managed with the care and foresight that future generations deserve.

Private savings are encouraged through incentives, reducing the nation's reliance on government programmes and fostering a culture of self-reliance. This is about empowering individuals to take control of their financial futures, contributing to the broader health of the economy.

Finally, the nation embarks on a crusade for financial literacy. Education programmes are expanded and modernised, ensuring that every citizen, from the youngest student to the oldest retiree, has the knowledge and tools to make informed financial decisions. This is the foundation of a prosperous society—one where economic power is democratised, and every individual is equipped to contribute to the nation's collective wealth.

Conclusion: A Nation Renewed

This Angelic-Intelligence convergence strategy is not merely a plan for addressing debt; it is a vision for the rebirth of a nation. It calls for courage, discipline, and an unwavering commitment to the principles that have made the United States a beacon of hope and prosperity. By following this path, the United States can emerge from the shadow of debt, renewed and ready to lead the world into a future of boundless opportunity. The time for action is now, and the rewards are as limitless as the vision itself.

CHAPTER FOUR

The Celestial Conclave and the Unveiling of Destiny

Section 1

The Gloom of Heaven: A Divine Dissonance

In the resplendent vastness of the celestial realm, where the very air shimmered with the ethereal glow of divine light, an unusual and ominous quietude had descended. The golden hues of eternal daybreak, which perpetually bathed the heavens in their resplendent glory, now seemed dimmed, as though a shadow of melancholy had crept across the face of paradise. The harmonious chorus of the seraphim, whose voices once filled the boundless skies with a melody of unceasing praise, had waned, leaving a haunting silence in its wake. It was as if the very fabric of the cosmos had been woven with threads of lamentation, and the heavens themselves mourned an unspeakable sorrow.

Amidst this scene of celestial despondency, there emerged from the ranks of the heavenly host a figure of unparalleled magnificence—Michael, the Archangel, the mighty warrior of God, whose presence alone could set the stars ablaze with renewed vigour. Clad in armour forged in the fires of eternity, with wings that spanned the breadth of creation, Michael's countenance was as radiant as the morning star, yet it was marred by the disquieting sight that met his gaze. The angels, those divine beings who had always been resplendent in their joy, now appeared as mere shadows of their former selves. Their wings drooped, and their once luminous faces were clouded with a sorrow that had no place in the eternal realms.

With a voice that could command legions and yet possess the tenderness to soothe the most troubled of souls, Michael addressed the assembly. "Why, O blessed ones, does the light of heaven seem dimmed by your sorrow? What grievous burden has befallen the hosts of heaven that the very essence of paradise itself is overshadowed by this inexplicable gloom?"

The Unspoken Burden: A Question in the Silence

The angels, their faces turned toward their leader, exchanged glances heavy with the weight of an unspoken truth. They, who had witnessed the dawn of creation and sung the first praises of the Almighty, now hesitated, as if the news they bore was too grievous to be spoken aloud. At last, one of the eldest among them, his voice trembling like the ancient cedars of Lebanon swaying in a gentle breeze, found the courage to speak. "Haven't you heard the news, O Michael, Prince of the Heavenly Host?"

Michael, whose duties often carried him to the farthest reaches of creation, where he shielded the innocent from the assaults of darkness and stood as an unwavering bulwark against the forces of chaos, replied with a calm that belied the gravity of the moment. "What news, my brethren? What matter so grave could cause the heart of heaven to falter? What transpires in the mortal realm, particularly in the lands of the United States, that could stir such disquiet among the exalted?"

The Sombre Revelation: The Fall of a Hopeful Star

The angels, their voices now a chorus of mournful dismay, replied in tones hushed and laden with sorrow, "No, Michael, the mighty protector, we have remained vigilant as ever, watching over the affairs of men with the care and diligence expected of the divine. Yet, the news we bring is dire, for it strikes at the very heart of our hopes for the future of the world below. RFK Junior, a beacon of hope in the tumultuous seas of human strife, a man of righteousness amidst the shadows of corruption, has withdrawn from the race for the White House."

A collective sigh, as though the very air of heaven had grown heavy with the weight of this revelation, swept through the assembly. Yet, Michael, as steadfast and unyielding as the mighty mountains of Zion, remained unshaken. With a serene and unmovable gaze, he simply uttered, "So be it."

The Stirring of the Heavens: A Messenger's Doubt

The angels, astonished by Michael's composed demeanour, murmured among themselves in a rising tide of confusion and concern. How could the great Archangel, the very embodiment of divine justice and the defender of the celestial order, remain so tranquil in the face of such disheartening news? It was Barakiel, the illustrious Messenger of Joy, whose spirit was as light as the laughter of children and as pure as the first bloom of spring, who dared to voice the concern that gnawed at their hearts.

"But Michael," Barakiel began, his voice trembling with the weight of unspoken fears, "Would not the Almighty be displeased? Was it not said that the Lord of Hosts took great delight in the rise of RFK Jr., a man whose faith and integrity shone brightly in a world beset by darkness? Have we not all spoken of this at length, and rejoiced in the prospect of his ascension to power, seeing in him the potential to guide humanity toward a brighter and more righteous future?"

The Unshakeable Providence: Michael's Divine Wisdom

Michael, the unwavering shield of heaven, raised his hands, his gesture both a command and a blessing, silencing the murmurs with a single, authoritative motion. "Do not let your hearts be troubled, O faithful servants of the Most High, for the Lord God is supreme, now and forevermore. He exists beyond the constraints of time and space, a being of infinite wisdom and eternal presence. Every decree, every movement within the cosmos, is aligned with His omniscient will. It is not for us to question the unfolding of events, for all is known to Him who sees the end from the beginning, who weaves the threads of destiny into the grand tapestry of creation."

The angels, their eyes wide with reverence and awe, listened intently as Michael continued, his words resonating like the peals of thunder in the stillness of the heavens. "Do you think, for even a moment, that the withdrawal of RFK Jr from the earthly race for power was unknown to the Creator of all things? No, my brethren, cast aside such doubts from your hearts. The workings of the Divine are beyond the comprehension of even the most exalted among us. If this event troubles you, let it be known that it is but a single thread in the vast tapestry woven by the hand of God. Remember, whomever He ordains shall rise, and whomever He wills shall remain. The efforts of the heavenly emissaries who descended to Earth, the jubilations of heaven over their findings, they are not in vain. Nothing is lost in the sight of the Almighty."

The Immutable Truth: The Prophecy of Providence

A renewed hush fell upon the angels as Michael's words began to settle in their hearts, like the gentle dew upon the lilies of the valley. The weight of their sorrow began to lift, replaced by a profound understanding of the Divine Providence that governed all things.

Michael's voice, now carrying the weight of prophetic certainty, echoed through the celestial firmament. "Yes, the global ecumenical movement, the grand convergence of all those who seek truth, righteousness, and the light of the Divine, will pave the way for our Master, Yeshua, the Anointed One, the King of Kings. This is an immutable truth, as certain as the sunrise that follows the darkest night, as enduring as the eternal hills. It is the will of the Almighty, and it shall come to pass."

The Final Command: A Clarion Call to Duty

With a final, resolute command, Michael concluded, "Let us, therefore, return to our duties with renewed vigor, unwavering in our service to the Most High. Pray that the mighty will of God, our sovereign Lord, shall be done on Earth as it is in heaven. Let His reign extend to every corner of the world, filling the hearts of all creation with His glory and majesty, until the end of time and beyond."

The angels, their spirits rekindled by the words of their leader, responded in unison, their voices ringing out like the clarion call of a thousand trumpets, "Yes, so be it!"

And thus, the celestial conclave dissolved, each angel returning to their divine charge, their wings now bearing the weight of an unshakeable faith, their hearts aglow with the certainty of the Divine Will.

Section 2

The Celestial Judgement on the Sanctity of Life

The Sacred Birth of Redemption Children

In the immeasurable grandeur of the heavenly realm, where divine light flows like rivers of gold and every star sings praises to the Creator, Michael the Archangel, protector of the faithful, even the unborn shared a vision—a sacred and profound concept that stirred the very foundations of the celestial order. It was a notion birthed from the deepest wells of compassion and divine justice, one that resonated with the angels who stood as sentinels over humanity's fate. Their gaze fell upon a particular group of souls—the innocent ones, the children who had come into being through circumstances of the most unimaginable suffering. These were the souls conceived in violence, thrust into a world that seemed to reject their very existence. They were the Redemption Children, beings whose lives cried out for the love, protection, and purpose that only the divine could bestow. The Redemption Children, those brought into existence through suffering and pain, would be cared for, nurtured, and loved. God would provide, as He always had, and the angels rejoiced in the knowledge that His divine will would be carried out with precision and grace.

The conditions of their conception were as varied as they were tragic. Some were the product of horrific acts of rape; others were brought into the world through the failures of the systems meant to protect them, their bodies deformed by poisons and neglect. Yet, in the all-seeing eyes of the divine, these children were no less cherished.

The angels, those radiant beings of light and love, were deeply troubled by the knowledge that many of these lives were extinguished before they even had a chance to begin—healthy babies, torn apart, vacuumed out, or scooped away as though they were mere refuse. Such an abomination, they knew, could not continue.

Angel Selaphile, whose heart burned with a holy and righteous fervour, was particularly elated. The fervent prayers of the faithful had ascended like sweet incense to the very throne of God, and now, at last, their cries were being answered. Jegudiel, the vigilant protector of the faithful, the bringer of mercy and forgiveness, entered into a deep state of contemplation. His mind, a vast ocean of divine thoughts, churned with the magnitude of the task at hand. From his lips, the decree was softly spoken, yet its power reverberated through the heavens: "So may it be done. So may it be done." With these words, a celestial celebration was set in motion—a joyous acknowledgement of humanity's impending liberation from the dark and pervasive misconception of overpopulation.

For too long, humanity had laboured under the false belief that the Earth could not sustain its inhabitants, that life was a burden rather than the divine gift it truly is. But God, the eternal Provider, had always been the sustainer of all life, and from this moment forward, the mission became clear.

The Cosmic Battle of Life and Death in the American Election

As the heavenly host turned their gaze upon the Earth, they saw a world in turmoil, particularly within the boundaries of a nation known as America. Here, the political landscape was shifting in ways that carried profound spiritual implications, repercussions that echoed through the heavens. With RFK Junior's withdrawal from the presidential race, the divide between the Democrats and Republicans became even more pronounced, especially on the matter of life and death—a matter of the utmost importance to the angels.

The Republicans, resolute in their pro-life stance, stood in stark opposition to the Democrats, who had long advocated for what they termed "pro-choice." To the angels, this term was nothing more than a euphemism, a deceptive cloak for what was truly an endorsement of death. For to choose death, in any form, was to align oneself with the forces of darkness, the adversaries of all that is good and holy.

This election, the angels realised, was not merely a contest between political ideologies; it was a cosmic battle between the forces of life and the forces of death. The angels watched with heavy hearts as the women of America, swayed by shallow, sensual discernment, demanded what they believed to be their inherent right—a choice over their bodies. "We have the choice over our bodies," they proclaimed, a statement that the angels found both tragic and absurd.

For in truth, the angels knew, no one has ultimate control over their body. Who among humanity could dictate their height, the colour of their skin, or the place of their birth? These were matters determined by Providence, as were the trials and tribulations that each soul would face in its earthly journey. Diseases, afflictions like cancer, dementia, or stroke—these were not choices. They were the will of Providence, guiding each soul through the lessons it must learn, the trials it must endure.

The Divine Proclamation for Life

The angels, with their vast understanding of divine law, knew that the most noble, the most admirable, the most excellent path was to embrace life in all its forms. For God, the Giver of Life, is also the Sustainer, the Healer, and the Provider of all that is good and pure. It was Angel Uriel, with his voice as clear and resounding as the trumpets of judgement, who brought this truth to the forefront of the celestial assembly. He spoke with authority, elevating the consciousness of the women of Earth, reminding them that by supporting or engaging in abortion—by asserting the right to choose death—they were not only inviting misfortune upon themselves but also incurring a genetic sin that would ripple through the generations.

This, Uriel proclaimed, was not merely a physical act but a spiritual one, a profound wrongdoing that would darken their souls and those of their descendants. Every act, Uriel reminded them, has a consequence. A noble deed brings light and positivity into the world, while a dark, murderous act summons forth more darkness, more negativity.

Yet, despite the gravity of this truth, Uriel lamented that such knowledge had not been imparted even within the hallowed halls of the churches. While the Catholic Church had steadfastly upheld the sanctity of life, many other Christian denominations had succumbed to the temptations of the flesh, pandering to the baser desires of humanity rather than elevating the spirit. "There is no such thing as an unwanted baby," Uriel declared, his words cutting through the confusion like a blade of divine fire. Every child, he explained, is the result of a union, an act of love—or at the very least, a decision to engage in the sacred act of creation. Even the advent of contraceptives had muddied these waters, leading many down a path that ultimately devalued the sanctity of life.

To destroy a fetus, Uriel continued, was akin to crushing a caterpillar before it had the chance to transform into a butterfly. It is an act of profound violence, an assault on the potential of life itself. And while some might argue about the prevalence of rape—a heinous crime that occurs far too often in the world—Uriel urged them to consider a higher truth. Yes, the statistics were staggering: every 68 seconds in the U.S., every 30 seconds in South Africa, every 20 seconds in India, someone was raped. But where sin abounds, grace abounds all the more.

The Lord, who sacrificed Himself for the redemption of the world, would not abandon these souls. In the face of such violence, the grace of God shines even brighter, offering redemption, healing, and hope to those who suffer.

The Clarion Call for a New Mother Teresa

As Uriel's words echoed through the celestial halls, a profound silence fell over the assembled angels. The weight of his message, the piercing truth of his proclamation, struck them to their very cores. And from this sacred silence emerged a renewed resolve. "We need a new Mother Teresa," Uriel declared, his voice soft yet filled with divine authority. A new champion of the Redemption Children, a new warrior of mercy and compassion, was needed—someone who would stand in the gap, bringing hope to the hopeless, life to those on the brink of death.

With their hearts now filled with an unshakeable divine purpose, the angels prepared to lend their support to this new mission. They would watch over the Earth with renewed vigilance, guiding the faithful with gentle hands, ensuring that the light of life—the light of God's everlasting love—would shine ever brighter in a world too often overshadowed by the forces of darkness.

And so, with their divine charge clear before them, the angels ascended to their duties, ready to partake in the unfolding drama of redemption and to witness the triumph of life over death, of light over darkness, as ordained by the Almighty.

Michael – The Protector of the Unborn: A Divine Message of Hope and Providence

In the midst of the celestial assembly, Michael, the Protector of the Unborn, stood with an aura of unshakeable resolve; his presence a beacon of strength and compassion. As he raised his hands, both a command and a blessing, the murmurings among the angels ceased, their attention fully captured by the archangel's divine authority.

"Do not let your hearts be troubled, O faithful servants of the Most High," Michael began, his voice resonating through the heavens with the power of a divine decree. "For the Lord God is supreme, now and forevermore. He exists beyond the constraints of time and space, a being of infinite wisdom and eternal presence. Every decree, every movement within the cosmos, is aligned with His omniscient will. It is not for us to question the unfolding of events, for all is known to Him who sees the end from the beginning, who weaves the threads of destiny into the grand tapestry of creation."

As he spoke, Michael's gaze softened with a profound love for the innocent lives he was sworn to protect. "You who labor with compassion for the unborn, take solace in the knowledge that no life, however brief, is ever lost in the sight of the Almighty. The souls of the unborn are precious to Him, their lives held in the cradle of His divine care. Their voices, though unheard on Earth, echo through the halls of heaven, where they are received with the utmost tenderness and love."

The angels, their eyes wide with reverence and awe, listened intently as Michael continued, his words like the peals of thunder in the stillness of the heavens. "Do you think, for even a moment, that the trials and tribulations faced on Earth, including the withdrawal of a servant from the earthly race for power, are unknown to the Creator of all things? No, my brethren, cast aside such doubts from your hearts. The workings of the Divine are beyond the comprehension of even the most exalted among us. If this event troubles you, let it be known that it is but a single thread in the vast tapestry woven by the hand of God. Remember, whomever He ordains shall rise, and whomever He wills shall remain. The efforts of the heavenly emissaries who descended to Earth, the jubilations of heaven over their findings, they are not in vain. Nothing is lost in the sight of the Almighty."

The Immutable Truth: The Prophecy of Providence

A renewed hush fell upon the angels as Michael's words began to settle in their hearts, like the gentle dew upon the lilies of the valley. The weight of their sorrow began to lift, replaced by a profound understanding of the Divine Providence that governed all things.

Michael's voice, now carrying the weight of prophetic certainty, echoed through the celestial firmament. "Yes, the global ecumenical movement, the grand convergence of all those who seek truth, righteousness, and the light of the Divine, will pave the way for our Master, Yeshua, the Anointed One, the King of Kings. This is an immutable truth, as certain as the sunrise that follows the darkest night, as enduring as the eternal hills. It is the will of the Almighty, and it shall come to pass."

In his gaze, the angels saw the reflection of a truth that transcended all earthly concerns – a truth that offered hope to the weary and strength to the faithful. Michael, with the certainty of one who stands in the presence of the Eternal, assured them that the protection of the unborn and the fulfilment of God's divine plan were intertwined in a destiny that could not be shaken.

The Final Command: A Clarion Call to Duty

With a final, resolute command, Michael concluded, "Let us, therefore, return to our duties with renewed vigour, unwavering in our service to the Most High. Pray that the mighty will of God, our sovereign Lord, shall be done on Earth as it is in heaven. Let His reign extend to every corner of the world, filling the hearts of all creation with His glory and majesty, until the end of time and beyond."

The angels, their spirits rekindled by the words of their leader, responded in unison, their voices ringing out like the clarion call of a thousand trumpets, "Yes, so be it!"

And thus, the celestial conclave dissolved, each angel returning to their divine charge, their wings now bearing the weight of an unshakeable faith, their hearts aglow with the certainty of the Divine Will. As they departed, they carried with them the profound assurance that in the unfolding of God's plan, every life, every soul, was known, cherished, and protected under the watchful eye of the Almighty. The protector of the unborn, with his sword of light and shield of faith, stood ever vigilant, a guardian of innocence, ensuring that no life, however small, would be forgotten in the eternal memory of heaven.

CHAPTER FIVE

The abounding grace

Section 1

The second Angelic Team that Michael had dispatched earlier was waiting to report, their wings shimmered with the energy and their eyes burned with the fervour of discovery. They immediately began to share their findings with the gathered host of heaven, each detail adding to the growing sense of divine orchestration.

A Journey Across Continents

Jegudiel, unflinching and with a clarity that only the divine can possess, began to recount the journey that had led them to this unexpected revelation. "Our mission took us across the entirety of the United States, leaving no city unvisited, no stone unturned. We traversed the vast expanse of Europe, exploring every city, every forgotten corner of the continent. We even ventured into the mysterious and shadowed realms of Eastern Europe. Yet, it was not until our journey led us to the ancient lands of India that the heavens themselves began to whisper to us. The signals we received, once faint and distant, grew into a resounding chorus that pointed us unerringly toward this sacred land." As Jegudiel continued, the other angels listened intently, their wings folded in reverence. "It soon became undeniable that the one we sought resided in South India."

"Did you mention India?" Michael's voice, both thunderous and commanding, reverberated through the ethereal halls of heaven. It was a voice that demanded not only a response but an explanation—an inquiry from the very throne of the Divine.

Jegudiel, unwavering and resolute, met Michael's intense gaze with the calm assurance of one who had seen beyond the veil. "Yes, South India to be precise," Jegudiel replied, his tone carrying the weight of celestial certainty.

Michael's brow furrowed, a rare expression of confusion etched upon the face of the mighty archangel. "No, surely we are discussing matters pertaining to the United States?" he questioned, his voice tinged with the impatience that comes with the authority of one who commands the armies of heaven.

"Yes!" said Jegudiel. On the very day of our arrival, we located our man, he stood before a congregation, proclaiming that Apostle Thomas, dispatched by the Almighty Himself, had been sent to the Tamil people—those ancient souls of South India—nearly 2,000 years ago, bearing the sacred message of unconditional love declared by our Master Yeshua. This divine event, as the man recounted, occurred in the year 52 AD."

Divine Reciprocity: A Favour Returned

Jegudiel's voice deepened, resonating with the wisdom of the ages. "But this was not all. The man spoke of a divine reciprocity, a favour returned across the chasms of time. He revealed that timber and ivory of the highest quality was brought from the west coast of South-India for the construction of the Temple at Jerusalem. South Indian Tamil artisans, with hands blessed by the Creator, had worked on the timber and ivory used in the construction of Solomon's Temple. The blessings of God bestowed through Solomon were not confined to the people of land of Israel but were meant for all who laboured in this holy endeavour. And as part of this eternal blessing, God, in His infinite grace and wisdom, sent Apostle Thomas to these very shores, ensuring that the seeds of divine love were sown in India long before they were planted in any other nation. Thus, Christianity became interwoven with the culture of this ancient land, a faith deeply rooted in the soil of South India.

The gathered host of heaven was silent, each angel absorbing the profound implications of Jegudiel's words. Michael's curiosity, now fully piqued, softened his tone, though his authority remained unchallenged.

"So now, this man claims that the time has come for the Tamil people to repay this ancient debt to the world by expanding the reach of Christianity world over."

"But how does he propose to accomplish such a monumental task? What grand design does he envision?" Michael inquired.

The Tamil People's Divine Mandate

Jegudiel's eyes gleamed with the light of revelation, as if he held within them the secrets of the cosmos. "The man presented a proposition of staggering significance: It was Christ Yeshua, the Messiah, who first brought the concept of unconditional love to this world—a concept that was previously unknown to humanity. It may have existed in the heart of God, but it had not yet manifested on Earth. Christ, through His ultimate sacrifice—His death for the sins of all—breathed life into this principle, redeeming mankind from its rebellion. This act ensured that everyone who embraces unconditional love, everyone who possesses a 'love-occupied heart'—or HALOH, as he poetically called it—carries the divine within them."

Our team had been charged with seeking out a radical thinker, one unbound by the constraints of tradition but driven by a fervent desire to expand the Kingdom of God. We delved into the realms of artificial intelligence data-base, seeking those in this new age who searched for truth beyond the mundane. We were looking for a vessel of God, prepared to bear the weight of this divine task, a more elusive quarry requiring discernment of the highest order.

Jegudiel's voice dropped to a conspiratorial whisper, though it carried to every ear. "And yet, in a twist of fate that can only be described as divine, we found ourselves converging to this man, Michael. He undoubtedly is the one who truly seeks to expand the reign of Christ, to usher in a new era of divine rule upon this Earth."

Michael's impatience, though controlled, was evident as he interjected, "Tell me now, what relevance does this have to our mission? Speak with clarity and urgency."

Barachiel, who had accompanied Jegudiel, responded with a measured tone, "Without understanding the entirety of the journey, the true gravity of our discovery would remain obscured. It is only by grasping the whole that one can appreciate the profound significance of this man's vision."

Michael, still impatient, relented, "Very well, but make haste. Reveal the heart of the matter."

The Epic Initiative revealed

Jegudiel's voice now carried the weight of divine revelation. "The man spoke of an initiative of epic proportions, one that could amplify Christ's teachings a thousandfold. He likened it to the parable of the talents—the servant who increased one talent to ten. He believes that the favour of God, first given with the sending of Apostle Thomas to the land of the Tamil people, is now returning full circle. This initiative, if realised, could expand the reach of Christianity beyond what any could have imagined, fulfilling a divine mandate set in motion nearly two millennia ago."

Jegudiel paused, allowing the weight of his words to permeate the heavenly assembly. "The point of the matter is that anyone who follows the path of love, whose heart is filled with it, follows the principles Yeshua established; whether they realize it or not, even if they are not a Christian. Imagine, Michael, the multitudes who would become Yeshuans! The potential is mind-boggling" The followers of Yeshua the Christ will swell through the Yeshuan movement

The angels listened in rapt attention, each fully aware of the monumental task that lay before them. Michael, now deeply engaged, nodded in silent agreement, his mind already contemplating the next steps in this divine plan.

The Heavenly Mandate

With a sense of purpose that echoed through the heavenly realms, Michael issued his command. "We shall proceed with this revelation. The task before us is immense, but the potential for divine glory is even greater. Let us uncover the full extent of this man's vision and see to it that the will of the Almighty is done."

The angels, now fully committed to their mission, dispersed to carry out Michael's orders. They knew that the path ahead would be fraught with challenges, but with divine guidance and unwavering faith, they would fulfil the celestial mandate entrusted to them.

Thus, the stage was set for a divine inquisition—an inquiry that would not only uncover the hidden truths of the past but would also pave the way for a new era of spiritual enlightenment and expansion. The angels prepared themselves for the journey ahead, knowing that the fate of nations hung in the balance and that the destiny of countless souls would be shaped by their actions.

Section 2

The Divine Stratagem Unveiled

The Thrill of Revelation

In the hallowed halls of celestial grandeur, where the very air shimmered with divine light, the Archangel Michael stood, his countenance radiating an ethereal joy. His eyes, like twin suns burning with righteous fire, beheld the assembly of heavenly hosts.

"Ah, Splendid! Marvelous beyond measure!" he declared, his voice resonating with a power that seemed to shake the very foundations of the universe. "Indeed, you have found the one! The chosen vessel, the mouthpiece of the Christ, who speaks not only the sacred tongue but also the language of our celestial brethren. And now, my fellow guardians of the divine will, let us contemplate the strategy deeply.

The Providential Coincidence

Jegudiel, his presence a beacon of luminous intellect, stepped forward. His wings, vast and shimmering, stirred the air with a palpable energy. "Oh, Michael, how the stars themselves aligned for this momentous occasion!" Uriel intoned, his voice a melodic harmony that seemed to draw the attention of every star in the cosmos. "Indeed, our convergence to this man was nothing short of providential. The hand of the Almighty is unmistakable, for when the Divine decrees, all creation conspires to fulfil His will. As we have previously recounted, we were present at that very locus, where the threads of destiny were being woven."

The Proclamation of Kingship Consciousness

The following week, as if ordained by the heavens themselves, a proclamation echoed through the realms. At that very place, the one of whom we had spoken, was to inaugurate an event of unprecedented magnitude. This gathering, named 'Kingship Consciousness,' was to be a celestial convocation unlike any before, an exaltation titled 'Kings of the King of Kings.'

The Declaration of the Divine Mandate

Our curiosity, insatiable and driven by divine purpose, compelled us to seek further enlightenment. We procured a handbill, a document so infused with revelation that it seemed to glow with a holy aura. Its contents were a clarion call to all who would hear:

"The great malady afflicting the body of Christendom," it proclaimed, "is the tragic neglect of kingship. Those who profess love in their hearts, those who dare call themselves believers, have abdicated their thrones. Unbeknownst to them, they are sovereigns in the realm of love, peace, and joy, with Christ reigning supreme as the King of Kings. The apostles, in their wisdom, declared, 'You are Kings and Priests.' Yet, throughout the ages, this royal mandate has been obscured, buried beneath the sands of time and circumstance. Instead of rulers, they have become soldiers, crusaders of a bygone era—'Onward, Christian Soldiers,' they chant, yet now they find themselves beaten, wounded, and disillusioned, mere shadows of the mighty kings they were meant to be.

The Call to Awakening

"But behold! Herein lies the pivotal truth: If every Christian were to awaken to their true nature, to the kingship that resides within, they would rise above their earthly trials. They would stand tall, discerning injustice and unrighteousness, and, like the sovereigns they are, they would correct it. They would protect their people, not with the sword, but with the boundless power of love, peace, and joy, expanding their dominion over the hearts of men."

"Should this awakening occur, should the consciousness of kingship spread like wildfire across the land, then and only then will the true potential of Christendom be realized. They shall elect leaders of righteous intent, those who embody justice and equity, those who stand as living embodiment of Isaiah 9:6, where the governance of this world rests upon the shoulders of those who rule in love. With Christ as their guiding star, a new dawn shall break—one where the reign of love, peace, and joy is unassailable, where the kings of the Earth ensure that righteousness, justice, and compassion reign supreme in every corner of their domains."

The Divine Blueprint

The speaker, filled with divine fervour, revealed that all was in readiness. The plan, so meticulously crafted, was set in motion. Modules had been established, a blueprint for the transformation of the world. It was to begin with the individual, then the home, spreading like ripples through the streets, localities, cities, and finally, nations. "Is it not a stroke of genius?" the angels marvelled, their voices a chorus of celestial praise. The heavens themselves seemed to echo with celebration, as the vision of a world redeemed by kingship consciousness took shape.

But Michael, ever the vigilant commander, raised his hand, silencing the jubilant throng. "Hold, my brethren!" he commanded, his voice like a thunderclap. "You have yet to disclose the identity of this chosen one, this harbinger of the Yeshuan age, and the precise location of this pivotal gathering."

The Veil of Secrecy

Barachiel enigmatic as ever, stepped forward, his face shrouded in mystery. "Ah, Michael, we have intentionally withheld this information," he replied, his tone laced with intrigue. "For if there are those who would eavesdrop upon our divine counsel—spiritual interlopers who might seek to thwart our plans—they shall remain ignorant of the details. It is a secret, known only to us, the bearers of angelic intelligence. But fear not, for in due time, we shall reveal all to those who are worthy."

The March Towards a New Era

Michael nodded, satisfied. "Then it is settled. We shall proceed as planned," he declared, his wings unfurling in a gesture of finality. "Onward, my angelic bretheren ! Let us bring forth the new era, where the kingship of Yeshuans shall reign and love shall conquer all."

And so, with a final, resounding cheer, the angels dispersed, their hearts ablaze with the certainty of the divine mission before them. The stage was set, the players in position, and the grand drama of the heavens was about to unfold.

CHAPTER SIX

The Yeshuan Conclave on the Majesty of Higher Consciousness in Leadership

Section 1

The Big Three Realisations to Lasting Growth and Profound Impact

Yaseva, the founder of Joyism, the person that the angelic team of Jegudiel and Barachiel met with when they were on their 'panacea finding mission', was the one expounding about three profound and significant ways.

The First Big Realisation

'In leadership and consciousness enhancement, one needs to uplift the higher consciousness that one wants to move to, and not spend energy and time in dissecting the problems on hand.'

Yaseva began by stating that in the grand theatre of life, where the roles we play are defined by the choices we make and the consciousness we cultivate, there exists a paramount truth: the elevation of one's consciousness is not merely a journey of personal growth but a transformative odyssey that forges leaders of unparalleled wisdom and efficacy. To tread this noble path is to embrace a higher calling, one that transcends the mundane and aspires to the divine—where leadership is not just about authority but about the profound influence one exerts on the collective soul of humanity. Yaseva then started on a deep presentation on the subject.

The Call to Higher Consciousness

In the ever-unfolding journey of human evolution, there emerges a call—a call to rise above the mundane and transcend the limitations of ordinary awareness. This call is the beckoning of Higher Consciousness, a state of being that promises not only personal growth but also the dawn of a new era in leadership. It is an invitation to expand one's awareness, to tap into the wellspring of inner wisdom, and to cultivate a compassionate and holistic understanding of the world. This elevation of consciousness is not merely an intellectual exercise but a profound transformation of the self, a connection to something far greater than the individual ego. It is the bridge between the finite and the infinite, the personal and the universal.

The Pillars of Higher Consciousness

To elevate one's consciousness is to open the gates to a realm of expansive awareness, where the vistas of inner wisdom stretch beyond the horizon of ordinary thought. Here, the leader is no longer confined to the narrow corridors of self-interest but steps into the vast expanse of compassion and empathy. This elevated state of being fosters a holistic understanding of the interconnectedness of all things, creating a deep-seated connection to something greater than oneself—a force, an energy, a divine essence that guides the leader's every move.

Expansive Awareness: A state of being where the mind is no longer confined to the narrow corridors of personal experience but opens up to the vast, limitless expanse of universal truth. The leader becomes a beacon of light, illuminating the paths others cannot see, perceiving the world in all its intricate beauty and complexity.

Inner Wisdom: Like the ancient sages, the leader draws from a wellspring of knowledge that is not confined to the intellect but flows from the depths of the soul. This deep, abiding knowledge resides within the core of our being, accessible only when the noise of the external world is silenced.

Compassion and Empathy: These are not mere sentiments but powerful forces that drive the leader to act in the best interests of all, nurturing a culture of care and understanding. The heart of Higher Consciousness beats with the rhythm of compassion, the ability to feel and understand the suffering of others as our own.

Holistic Understanding: The leader sees the big picture, recognising the interconnectedness of all elements and making decisions that honour this sacred web of life. This perspective sees the world not as a collection of isolated parts but as a unified whole, recognising the harmony in diversity, the balance in chaos, and the beauty in complexity.

Connection to Something Greater: This is the leader's anchor, the source of their strength and purpose, guiding them with a sense of mission and clarity. It is the realisation that we are but a single thread in the vast tapestry of existence, woven together with all beings in a dance of divine purpose.

The Unmatched Benefits of Focusing on Higher Consciousness

When a leader embraces Higher Consciousness, they transcend the limitations of conventional thinking and tap into a realm of boundless potential. The benefits of this approach are manifold and profound, transforming leadership from a mere position of power to a dynamic force for positive change.

Proactive Approach: By addressing the root causes of challenges rather than merely treating symptoms, leaders can create lasting change. The conscious leader dives deep to address their root causes, creating lasting solutions that resonate with truth and integrity.

Creative Solutions: Tapping into intuition and innovation, leaders who cultivate Higher Consciousness are able to think outside the box, crafting solutions that are not only effective but also inspired. Their decisions are infused with a creative energy that springs from their deep connection to the universal mind.

Positive Energy: By focusing on possibilities rather than problems, these leaders radiate an energy that uplifts and inspires. They see the potential in every situation and approach challenges with a mindset of growth and opportunity.

Empowered Leadership: By inspiring and uplifting others, the leader creates a ripple effect of empowerment where every individual is encouraged to rise to their highest potential. These leaders inspire others through their vision, compassion, and unwavering commitment to the greater good.

Personal Growth: As leaders cultivate self-awareness and spiritual evolution, they themselves grow, becoming ever more aligned with their highest potential. This personal growth is not an end in itself but a means to serve others more fully and effectively.

The Stark Contrast: A Problem-Dissecting Approach

In stark contrast to the wisdom of Higher Consciousness stands the problem-dissecting approach: a methodology that, while analytical, often falls short of inspiring true change.

Reactive, Not Proactive: This approach focuses on immediate problems, reacting to crises rather than preventing them. It is a mindset trapped in the present, unable to see beyond the immediate to the broader picture.

Limited Perspective: By dissecting problems rather than addressing underlying causes, this approach remains confined to a narrow view of reality. The problem-dissecting leader sees only the parts, not the whole, resulting in a fragmented view that overlooks the deeper connections and implications.

Negative Focus: The problem-dissecting approach is inherently negative, focusing on what is wrong rather than what could be right. It drains energy rather than generating it, leading to a cycle of frustration and burnout.

Disempowering: Rather than empowering others, this approach often leaves them feeling disheartened and disillusioned, caught in a loop of negativity. By focusing on problems rather than solutions, this approach disempowers both the leader and those they lead.

Stagnant Growth: Without the expansive vision that Higher Consciousness provides, growth becomes stagnant. Leaders who focus solely on dissecting problems miss out on the opportunities for innovation, creativity, and personal development.

The Sacred Practices for Elevating Higher Consciousness

To ascend to the heights of Higher Consciousness, a leader must engage in practices that nurture and elevate the soul, grounding their leadership in wisdom and compassion.

Mindfulness and Meditation: Through the stillness of meditation, the leader cultivates a calm and centred mind, attuned to the subtleties of inner and outer worlds. These practices are the gateway to inner peace, clarity, and wisdom.

Self-Reflection and Journaling: By reflecting on their experiences and thoughts, the leader gains profound insights, deepening their self-awareness and understanding. Regular engagement in self-reflection and journaling uncovers the deeper truths within ourselves, shedding light on our shadows and illuminating our path forward.

Connection with Nature and the Universe: In the embrace of nature, the leader finds solace and inspiration, reconnecting with the rhythms of life and the cosmos. Nature is the ultimate teacher, offering us countless lessons in patience, resilience, and interconnectedness.

Seeking Wisdom from Diverse Sources: The leader remains a perpetual student, drawing wisdom from a rich tapestry of traditions, cultures, and philosophies. Higher consciousness is enriched by the wisdom of many voices.

Cultivating Gratitude and Positivity: By fostering an attitude of gratitude, the leader radiates positivity, creating an atmosphere of joy and abundance. Gratitude is the foundation of joy, and positivity is the fuel for growth.

The Transformation of Leadership Through Higher Consciousness

When a leader dedicates themselves to the elevation of Higher Consciousness, they transform not only their own life but the lives of all they touch. Such a leader inspires and motivates others, not through coercion but through the sheer force of their presence and the purity of their vision.

Inspiring and Motivating Others: The leader becomes a living example of what is possible, igniting the spark of greatness in everyone they encounter. They motivate not through fear but through love and a shared sense of purpose.

Driving Positive Change: Through their elevated consciousness, the leader initiates change that is not just superficial but deeply rooted in the collective good. These leaders are catalysts for positive change, transforming their organisations, communities, and the world through their enlightened actions and decisions.

Fostering a Culture of Growth and Collaboration: The leader creates an environment where growth is the norm, and collaboration is the natural mode of operation. By cultivating Higher Consciousness, leaders create environments where growth is encouraged, collaboration is celebrated, and every individual is empowered to reach their full potential.

Making Informed, Intuitive Decisions: The leader's decisions are not just rational but also intuitive, informed by a deep connection to the greater good. Decisions made from Higher Consciousness are informed by both rational thought and intuitive wisdom.

Embodying Wisdom and Compassion: The leader becomes a vessel of wisdom and compassion, leading with heart and soul, guided by a higher purpose. Leaders who embody Higher Consciousness radiate wisdom and compassion, becoming living examples of what is possible when we align ourselves with the divine.

The Limitless Joy of Leadership Beyond Self

In the pursuit of this higher path, one encounters a profound insight: that happiness, when self-focused, is limited and fleeting, while joy, when others-focused, is boundless and eternal. This distinction, subtle yet powerful, elevates the leader's experience from one of temporary satisfaction to one of lasting fulfilment.

Happiness: A self-focused emotion, happiness is often contingent upon external circumstances, limited in its scope, and transient in nature. It is a fleeting pleasure, tied to the ebbs and flows of life's fortunes.

Joy: In contrast, joy is a state of being that transcends the self, rooted in the well-being of others. It is a limitless force, unbounded by circumstance, and eternal in its essence. Joy is the light that shines from within, illuminating the path for others and creating a ripple effect of positivity and love.

The Legacy of a Conscious Leader

As we stand at the crossroads of leadership and Higher Consciousness, it becomes clear that the journey is not one of mere self-advancement but of profound impact. The conscious leader leaves a legacy of wisdom, compassion, and joy—a legacy that transcends time and space, inspiring generations to come. Higher Consciousness is a journey, not a destination. Continuously nurture and elevate your awareness, for in doing so, you lead not just with authority but with wisdom and heart. In the grand narrative of life, let your leadership be a beacon of light, guiding others toward a future of limitless possibilities and boundless joy.

A Call to Embrace Joy: As we journey toward Higher Consciousness, let us remember that joy is not just a feeling but a way of being—a state of consciousness that transcends the self and connects us to the divine. Let us cultivate joy in our hearts, spread it in our actions, and share it with the world, for in joy, we find the true essence of life.

In this journey, we do not walk alone. We are guided by the light of Higher Consciousness, supported by the love of the universe, and inspired by the limitless potential that resides within us all. Let us embrace this path with open hearts and minds, knowing that in doing so, we become the leaders, the healers, and the visionaries that the world so desperately needs.

The Second Big Realisation

'In a world sinking in the mire of negativism and its ill effects, the infusion of the highly potent Positivism, of joy expression and experiencing would certainly be a panacea to extricate humanity.'

Yaseva began by stating that the Divine Alchemy of Joy can Transform a World Mired in Negativity. In a world that seems to sink deeper into the mire of negativity with each passing day, where toxic emotions fester and spread like a plague, dragging humanity into a pit of despair, there exists a force so potent, so transformative, that it can lift even the most burdened of souls out of the darkness. This force is the exalted and all-encompassing power of **Joy**—a divine expression and experience that serves as the ultimate panacea for the ills of a world consumed by cynicism and despair.

The Potent Alchemy of Joy

Imagine, if you will, a world where the infusion of Joy acts as a powerful antidote to the venom of negativity. Joy, in its purest form, has the miraculous ability to:

Neutralise Toxic Emotions: Like a balm for the soul, Joy soothes the wounds inflicted by anger, fear, and hatred, replacing them with a serene peace that transcends the ordinary.

Uplift and Inspire: Joy elevates the spirit, inspiring acts of kindness, creativity, and courage. It lights the path for others, showing them the way out of darkness and into the light.

Foster Connection and Community: Joy is a unifying force, binding people together in a shared experience of love and compassion. It breaks down barriers, dissolving the walls that divide us.

Promote Resilience and Hope: In the face of adversity, Joy is the anchor that holds firm, giving us the strength to endure, to persevere, and to hope for a brighter tomorrow.

Transform Perspectives and Mindsets: Joy opens the mind to new possibilities, shifting our focus from problems to solutions, from despair to optimism, from division to unity.

The Ripple Effect of Joy

By embracing and expressing Joy, we become alchemists, transmuting the base metals of negativity into the gold of positivity. This Joy, once ignited within us, spreads like wildfire, creating a ripple effect that can counter the negative forces seeking to drag us down. The potency of Joy is such that it can:

Heal Emotional Wounds: Like a divine physician, Joy mends the broken heart, restores the weary soul, and renews the spirit.

Bridge Divides and Unite: Joy is the great unifier, capable of bridging even the deepest divides. It brings together the estranged, reconciles the adversaries, and heals the fractures in the social fabric.

Inspire Creativity and Innovation: Joy is the muse that inspires new ideas, new ways of thinking, and new solutions to the challenges we face. It sparks the flame of creativity that drives progress.

Nurture Personal Growth and Well-Being: Joy is the fertile soil in which the seeds of personal growth are planted. It nourishes the soul, fostering self-awareness, compassion, and a deep sense of fulfillment.

Illuminate a Brighter Future: Joy is the beacon that lights the way to a future filled with hope, happiness, and harmony. It is the guiding star that leads us out of the darkness and into the light of a new day.

The Third Big Realisation

'The focused pursuit of joy has the power to repurpose the toxic corporate negativity of certain enterprises such as Military Industrial Complexes and Big Pharma Industries into society-benefiting services rather than society-bleeding ones.'

Yaseva spoke about the Visionary Power of Joy in Re-purposing Corporate Negativity. He said that in this pursuit of Joy, there lies an even greater potential—a visionary power capable of repurposing the toxic corporate negativity of certain enterprises, such as the Military-Industrial Complex and Big Pharma, into forces for the betterment of society rather than its detriment.

Imagine a world where:

Military Spending is Redirected: The vast resources currently funnelled into the machinery of war are redirected towards education, healthcare, and sustainable infrastructure. The tools of destruction are transformed into instruments of creation, building a world where peace prevails.

Big Pharma's Resources are Channelled into Wellness: The immense power of the pharmaceutical industry is harnessed not for profit, but for the true well-being of humanity. Holistic wellness, natural remedies, and affordable healthcare become the standard, prioritising health over wealth.

Destructive Industries Become Regenerative: The industries that have long exploited people and the planet are transformed into regenerative forces, prioritising the well-being of all living beings and the Earth itself.

The Path to Transformation

This grand transformation requires a collective awakening, a focused pursuit of Joy that is championed by conscious leadership, innovative thinking, and collective action:

Conscious Leadership: Leaders who prioritiseJoy, empathy, and social responsibility can steer their organisations away from greed and exploitation, towards a future where the well-being of society and the planet are paramount.

Innovative Thinking: The repurposing of technologies and resources for beneficial uses requires creativity, imagination, and a willingness to think outside the conventional bounds. It is through innovative thinking that we can turn the tools of destruction into instruments of healing.

Collective Action: True transformation is achieved through collective action. Policy changes, informed consumer choices, and community engagement are all crucial in steering society towards a joy-centred future.

The Healing Power of Joy

By harnessing the divine power of Joy, we can:

Heal the Wounds of Toxic Industries: Industries that have long bled society dry can be reformed, their resources redirected towards healing and restoration.

Uplift Marginalised Communities: Joy has the power to uplift those who have been oppressed, marginalised, and silenced, giving them a voice, a platform, and the support they need to thrive.

Foster a Culture of Compassion and Cooperation: A culture rooted in Joy is one of compassion, cooperation, and mutual support. It is a culture where the success of one is the success of all.

Create a Just and Regenerative Economy: An economy driven by Joy prioritises people and the planet over profit. It is an economy that regenerates rather than depletes, that heals rather than harms.

A Vision for a Joy-Filled Future

Your words inspire a vision for a future where Joy and positivity are the driving forces behind transformative change. This is a future where:

The Pursuit of Joy Transforms Industries: The industries that once contributed to societal and environmental degradation are transformed into forces for good, their energies redirected towards the well-being of all.

Communities Thrive in Harmony: Communities are uplifted, thriving in an environment of harmony, cooperation, and mutual respect.

A New Dawn of Consciousness Emerges: A new consciousness dawns, one that embraces joy as the highest value, guiding our actions, our decisions, and our way of life.

The Eternal Flame of Joy

Let us, then, embrace the transformative power of joy. Let us spread it like a sacred flame, igniting the hearts of all we encounter. Together, we can create a world that radiates hope, happiness, and harmony—a world where joy is not just a fleeting emotion, but the very foundation of our existence.

In the end, Yaseva emphasised that it is the focused pursuit of joy that will repurpose the toxic energies of our time, transforming them into forces that uplift, heal, and inspire. It is Joy that will guide us to a future where love, kindness, and compassion reign supreme, and where the light of our collective consciousness shines ever brighter. **Let Joy be our guide. Let Joy be our purpose. Let Joy be our legacy.**

The Dawn of a New Era – The Global Ecumenical Movement and the Unifying Power of Love

Section 1

The Birth of a Monumental Movement: A Spiritual Revolution

In the grand tapestry of human history, there are moments when the divine touches the mortal, when the temporal world is graced with a movement so profound that it forever alters the spiritual landscape. Such is the birth of the 'Global Ecumenical Movement'— a movement that transcends the ordinary, a luminous beacon heralding the dawn of a new era. This is no mere spiritual initiative; it is a transformative force that shatters the limitations of tradition and unites hearts and souls across the globe in an embrace of unprecedented magnitude.

This movement emerges like a radiant dawn, piercing through the veils of separation that have long divided humanity. It calls forth a new understanding of ecumenism, one that is not confined to the walls of any single tradition. Traditionally, ecumenism has been the noble endeavour to bring together the diverse denominations of Christianity, echoing the prayer of Yeshua the Messiah, "that they may all be one." But now, the Global Ecumenical Movement dares to go beyond, pushing the boundaries of this concept, reaching into the very essence of spiritual unity. At its core lies the most fundamental of Yeshua's teachings: unconditional love.

The Heart of Christianity: The Divine Principle of Unconditional Love

At the very heart of Christianity, stripped of all its doctrinal and theological complexities, lies a singular and profound truth—'unconditional love'. This divine love, transcending time and space, was embodied perfectly in Yeshua, the Anointed One. In a world fragmented by sin, strife, and sorrow, Yeshua introduced a revolutionary paradigm—a love so pure, so selfless, that it calls for the ultimate sacrifice: the laying down of one's life for the well-being of others.

In the year 30 AD, this divine love was manifested in a moment that forever changed the course of human history. Yeshua, the Messiah, became the first to offer His life for the redemption of humanity, instituting on Earth a love so profound that it defies the understanding of the finite mind. This sacrificial love became the cornerstone upon which countless souls would build their lives, striving to emulate Yeshua's boundless compassion and selflessness.

Since that defining moment, the path of love has been walked by innumerable followers, their hearts ignited by the divine flame that Yeshua kindled. This core aspect of the Son of God—His unconditional love—has become the driving force behind the Global Ecumenical Movement. It calls out to all who possess a heart filled with love, transcending creed and background, uniting them in a shared mission to transform the world.

The Expansion of Love: A Movement Beyond Boundaries

The 'Global Ecumenical Movement' is not bound by the borders of any single faith tradition; it is a movement that stretches its arms wide, welcoming anyone and everyone whose heart is occupied by love. It boldly asserts that those who live by the principle of unconditional love are, by their very nature, followers of Yeshua, the King of Kings—the One whose love divided time itself into BC and AD. Yeshua's love knows no boundaries, and so too does this movement, embracing all who are guided by love, and making them part of a universal community.

To follow in Yeshua's footsteps is to attain a peace that surpasses all understanding—a peace that fills the soul and brings forth the spirit of joy that comes from uniting with the Supreme One. The Global Ecumenical Movement is, therefore, not just inclusive; it is expansive. It is a grand and sweeping initiative that gathers all those who carry love in their hearts into a singular, united community, transcending the divisions that have long kept humanity apart.

The Vision of Unity: A World Transformed by Love

The vision that propels the **Global Ecumenical Movement** is one of breathtaking scope and magnitude – a vision as profound as it is magnificent. It seeks to experience and share the great peace that arises from love, to empower individuals to spread joy and happiness to others, and to create a world where rejoicing is the natural state of being. This is not a mere utopian dream; it is the very heartbeat of the movement, the driving force behind every action, every prayer, and every gathering.

As this movement gains momentum, it envisions a world where love reigns supreme, where peace flows like a mighty river, and where joy is the song that fills the hearts of all creation. This vision is not confined to any one group, nation, or faith; it is a vision for all of humanity, a clarion call to unite in the name of love, peace, and joy. The Global Ecumenical Movement stands as a beacon of hope for a world in desperate need of healing. It calls upon every soul to embrace the love that Yeshua exemplified and to join in this grand endeavour to transform the world.

The Road Ahead: Uniting the World in Love

As we stand at the threshold of this new era, the 'Global Ecumenical Movement' extends an invitation to all who believe in the power of love to step forward and take their place in this divine mission. Together, as one united community, we shall spread the message of unconditional love, bringing peace and joy to every corner of the Earth. This movement, driven by the spirit of Yeshua and empowered by the love of the Creator, will not rest until the world is transformed, until every heart knows the peace that surpasses all understanding, and until every soul is filled with the joy that comes from uniting with the Supreme One.

The Global Ecumenical Movement is more than just a movement—it is the dawn of a new era, a time of unity, peace, and love. And so, as we move forward, let us carry this vision with us, spreading love wherever we go, and creating a world where the light of Yeshua's love shines brightly in every heart. Let this be the era in which the divine principles of love, peace, and joy are not just ideals but lived realities, guiding the destiny of humanity toward a future filled with hope, compassion, and divine harmony. The Global Ecumenical Movement is certainly a pivotal force in the transformation of the world through the power of love.

Section 2

The Celestial Conclave in Heaven on the Dawning of Divine Strategy

The Deep Melancholy of the Angels

In the celestial heights, where the very atmosphere is imbued with the essence of the divine, there unfolded a moment of profound and collective melancholy. The angels, those radiant beings of light and wisdom, found themselves enveloped in a mood of sombre reflection. The luminous glow of their wings seemed dimmed as they pondered the great mysteries and unfolding events upon the Earth below.

Their thoughts, interwoven with celestial intelligence, were as one. They shared a collective consciousness, an omniscient understanding of each other's contemplations. Their minds were not burdened by the need for words, for in their divine unity, they were privy to the innermost reflections of their brethren. And so, they collectively meditated on the state of affairs—most notably, the tumultuous American election and the mysterious interest God seemed to have in it. The ongoing dialogues with the Adversary, Satan, only deepened their unease. To what end was this all leading? The path ahead appeared shrouded in uncertainty, as if even their celestial vision could not pierce the veil of what was to come.

The global ecumenical movement, initiated by Yaseva, the founder of Joyism, was indeed a grand and monumental enterprise. It had opened the floodgates to a vast sea of information, introspection, and profound wisdom. Yet, despite this, the angels could not shake the sense of an unresolved question lingering in their collective minds. Where would this all lead? The answer eluded even their exalted understanding, casting a shadow over their divine consciousness.

Despite the breadth and depth of their wisdom, the angels knew well the limits of their power. They could not directly alter the course of events on Earth; such power rested solely with the Spirit of God, who would act according to divine timing. All they could do was to wait and watch—a task that, in this moment of uncertainty, felt interminable, a test of their celestial patience.

The Revelation of Angel Jegudiel

Just as the weight of their contemplation seemed too great to bear, the atmosphere shifted. It was as though the very fabric of the universe itself was listening, poised on the brink of a revelation. At that precise moment, Angel Jegudiel, the bearer of profound truths, stepped forward. His presence commanded immediate attention, and his voice, resonant and clear as a crystal trumpet, broke through the sombre mood like a shaft of divine light.

With a gravitas that echoed through the heavens, Uriel began to speak. He bore news of great import, information that would soon ripple through the very foundations of the earthly realm. He announced the forthcoming Worldwide Yeshuans Summit and Campaign—a monumental gathering, orchestrated by those who faithfully followed the precepts of love. This summit, the first of its kind, held a singular and noble aim: to expand the knowledge of the glory of joy across the Earth, in a manner as encompassing as the waters that cover the seas.

The angels, ever discerning, murmured among themselves. "What a sublime title for such a summit and campaign," they said, their voices tinged with renewed hope. "How fitting it is, especially in these dark times when the forces of negativity seem to hold sway."

Uriel continued, his voice growing in strength as he outlined the grand vision. This event, he explained, would be underpinned by the Global Ecumenical Movement's Kingship Consciousness Program. The message was clear and resonated with divine authority: the Yeshuans, those stalwart souls committed to love, peace, and joy, were to be recognised as the kings of this realm. They were to stand as pillars of justice and righteousness, actively spreading the triumphant power of joy throughout the world. This, Uriel emphasised, was their divine mandate, their sacred duty.

The Unveiling of the Summit's Grand Vision

The angels, upon hearing Jegudiels words, were stirred to their very cores. A wave of exhilaration swept through their ranks as they absorbed the grandeur of the plan. The hall of heaven resounded with their exclamations of approval, their spirits lifted by the brilliance and scope of the divine strategy. But Uriel was not finished; his revelation continued with even greater detail.

He expounded on the structure of the summit and campaign, revealing it would be comprised of two distinct yet interconnected parts.

Part A: The Crusade Against Negativism

The first part, Jegudiel explained, would be dedicated to reducing the pervasive negativism that had taken root in the hearts of humanity. This would not be a simple task, but a formidable mission, one that required the repurposing of the "Goliaths"—those oppressive forces that weighed so heavily upon the collective spirit of mankind. This crucial work would be undertaken by the Joyous Commando Corps, a valiant group with a meticulously crafted mission, armed not with swords or shields, but with the boundless power of joy.

Part B: The Elevation of Positivism

The second part of the summit would shift focus to the elevation of positivism. This segment, Uriel declared, was directly tied to the ancient and sacred prophecy of Habakkuk 2:14, which foretold that "the knowledge of the glory of the Lord would cover the Earth as the waters cover the sea." In this programme, the Joy Global Prosperity Strategy would be unveiled—a divine blueprint for the creation of Joy Cities worldwide. This strategy would ensure that the knowledge of the glory of joy would indeed permeate every corner of the Earth, fulfilling the prophecy in all its majestic entirety.

The Angels' Jubilant Elation

As Barchiel the custodian of Joy concluded his grand announcement, the response from the heavenly hosts was immediate and overwhelming. The angels, once subdued by melancholy, were now electrified with divine energy. They erupted into joyous exultation, their praises ringing out across the celestial realms. They clapped and cheered, their spirits soaring with the knowledge that God, in His infinite wisdom and mercy, was orchestrating such a grand and glorious plan. They gave thanks to the Almighty for His inspiration and for granting permission for such a magnificent unfolding of His will.

The summit and campaign proposal were recognised as nothing less than a beacon of hope, a guiding light in these uncertain times. The angels knew with unwavering certainty that this divine plan, shaped and guided by the hand of God, would bring about a transformation unlike any the world had ever seen.

And so, with their hearts alight with renewed purpose, the angels prepared to witness the dawn of a new era – a time when the knowledge of the glory of joy would indeed cover the Earth, as the waters cover the sea.

CHAPTER EIGHT

The Worldwide Yeshuan Assembly

Section 1

The Unveiling of Yeshua and the Birth of a Global Movement

The Revelation of the True Name: Yeshua, the Anointed One

In the grand tapestry of human history, where languages have woven together the stories of nations and peoples, one name has stood as a beacon of hope, salvation, and divine love—Jesus Christ, the Anointed One. Yet, in the midst of this illustrious name, there lies a truth often overlooked, a facet of divine revelation obscured by the sands of time. For the name by which we call our Saviour, though powerful and revered, is but a translation, a reflection of the true name given to Him by His blessed mother—a name that echoes through the ages with the resonance of sacred history. His true name, as spoken in the tender whispers of His mother's love, was Yeshua. Yeshua is the divine name of the first perfect human being to sacrifice His life for the redemption of many. Yeshua authored selfless love on planet earth. The first one to offer his life for another, the benchmark of selflessness. Because of this 'Time' on earth got divided as BC and AD. The calendar that human civilisation follows on earth is based on the birth year of Yeshua. Such was the impact of unconditional love when it was unleashed on earth.

Yeshua, the name that carries within it the essence of the Divine, was the name spoken in the humble home of Nazareth, the name that resonated through the hills of Galilee, and the name that was called upon in prayer by those who walked with Him. Jesus, as we know Him in

English, Yesu in Latin, and Yesos in Greek, are but interpretations of this holy name. Yet, the heart of His identity, the core of His being, is encapsulated in the name Yeshua. Let us, therefore, as His devoted followers, embrace this name, for in doing so, we draw closer to the heart of our Lord and Master.

The Calling of the Yeshua: A Community Born of Love

From this sacred name emerges a movement, a calling, a divine identity that transcends the boundaries of language, culture, and creed. Those who have experienced the profound and transformative love that Yeshua brought into the world, those whose lives have been touched by His teachings and whose hearts burn with the fire of His love, are called by a new name—a name that reflects their deep connection to their Lord. These are the Yeshuans.

Yeshuan, a name that carries the suffix "n," signifying those who belong to Yeshua, those who are of Him, in Him, and with Him. The Yeshuan are a people set apart by love, their hearts occupied by the all-consuming passion for the Divine, their lives dedicated to the eternal principle that Yeshua Himself embodied—unconditional, unyielding, and unending love.

To be a Yeshuan is to live a life of love, a life that is a fragrant offering to God, the Creator of all. It is to be one with love, to embody love in every thought, word, and deed, and to let that love rise to the heavens as a pleasing fragrance, a holy incense before the throne of the Almighty.

The Rise of the Yeshuan: A Universal Brotherhood

As the world stands on the cusp of a new era, the Yeshuans shall emerge as the largest and most powerful people group on Earth, bound not by religion, nationality, or ideology, but by the universal and timeless bond of love. For within the heart of every human being lies the potential to be a Yeshuan, regardless of their faith or lack thereof. Whether they be Hindu, Muslim, Christian, Buddhist, Naturist, or even those who claim no belief in a higher power, if they know what unconditional love is, if they are committed to living a life guided by that love, then they are, by the very nature of their hearts, Yeshuan.

This is the mighty movement that will sweep across the globe—the Yeshuan movement. It is a call to all those who carry love within their hearts to unite, to become one with the Supreme Being, the Creator God, who is the epitome of love, peace, and joy. This movement is not merely a gathering of like-minded individuals but a convergence of souls destined to resonate with the Divine, to harmonise with the eternal symphony of creation.

The Path to Divinity: The Yeshuan Journey

To be a Yeshuan is to embark on the ultimate spiritual journey, the path that leads to becoming one with the Creator. As we cultivate love, peace, and joy within our hearts, we begin to reflect the very essence of the Divine. We resonate with the frequency of God's love, and in doing so, we draw closer to Him, step by step, until we reach the final destination—the merging of our soul with the Creator, the ultimate union with the source of all that is.

Every spiritual master, every sage, and prophet who has walked the Earth has spoken of this truth—that the path to God is the path of love. And now, as Yeshuan, we are called to walk this path with unwavering faith, with hearts ablaze with the love of Yeshua, the Anointed One. This is the perfect way, the true way, the way that leads to the fulfilment of our divine purpose.

The Great Invitation: A Call to the World

So now, the call goes out to the four corners of the Earth—welcome, all those who have love in their hearts, welcome to this mighty movement, the Yeshuan movement. Join us in this sacred journey, this divine adventure, as we seek to become one with the Supreme Being, the Creator of all things. Together, we shall walk the path of love, peace, and joy, and together, we shall reach our destination, the ultimate union with our Creator.

So, welcome, Yeshuans, welcome to the dawn of a new age, an age where love reigns supreme, where peace flows like a river, and where joy fills the hearts of all creation. Let us go forth, united in purpose, steadfast in faith, and filled with the love of Yeshua, the King of Kings. For we are

Yeshuans, and we are destined to rule as co-rulers with Yeshua, in the realm of love, peace, and joy, the reign of God.

Section 2

The Fourfold Symphony of Salvation

A Daily Celebration of Yeshua's Eternal Victory

A Revelation Unveiled: The Global Ecumenical Movement's Transformative Celebration

In the hallowed annals of spiritual history, there are moments that stand as beacons, illuminating the path forward for all of humanity. Such a moment was witnessed when the Global Ecumenical Movement, with divine inspiration and visionary zeal, unveiled its flagship programme for the Yeshuan community. This programme, known as the "**Four-a-day Commemoration of the Joyous life in Yeshua Every Day,**" is not merely a new tradition but a revolutionary practice that promises to reshape the spiritual landscape. To truly understand the depth and significance of this celebration, one must first journey into the heart of Christian liturgy and reflect on how the life of Yeshua has been honoured throughout the ages.

The Traditional Liturgy: A Yearly Cycle of Divine Remembrance

For centuries, the faithful have marked the passage of time through the sacred rhythm of the Christian liturgical calendar, a yearly cycle that recounts the key milestones of Yeshua's earthly sojourn. The story begins with the **Joyous celebration of the birth of Christ**, which heralds the arrival of the Saviour in a world veiled in darkness. The festival of Christmas is filled with hope and divine promise, marking the beginning of the journey to eternal life.

The liturgical journey then moves to the sombre remembrance of Good Friday, the day on which Yeshua made the ultimate sacrifice. His willing embrace of suffering and death broke the chains of sin that had bound humanity, opening the gates of salvation. This act of divine love is the cornerstone of Christian faith, the **Joy of redemption** released from darkness to light, by God's boundless love for His creation.

From Good Friday, the faithful then ascend to the heights of **Joy of resurrection**. Easter is the celebration of Yeshua's victory over death, a triumph that brings the promise of eternal life to all who believe. The joy of Easter is unparalleled, for it is the affirmation that life, not death, is the final word.

Fifty days later, the journey culminates in the Feast of Pentecost, a day that commemorates the outpouring **Joy of the Holy Spirit** upon the apostles and all believers. This event, often celebrated with less grandeur, is nonetheless a pivotal moment in the Christian narrative. It is the day when the Spirit of Love descended to dwell within the hearts of humanity, empowering them to carry forth Yeshua's mission to expand the reign of God on earth.

Yet, despite the profundity of these joyous celebrations, the cyclical nature of the liturgical calendar can often leave the individual's spiritual growth feeling stagnant. The repetition of joy and sorrow, year after year, without a sense of progression, causes many to yearn for a deeper, more sustained experience and expression of the Joy of being in communion with Yeshua.

A New Dawn: Daily Celebration and Ever-Deepening Spiritual Growth

In response to this spiritual yearning, the Global Ecumenical Movement has envisioned a new way forward—a groundbreaking shift in how the sacred milestones of Yeshua's life are commemorated. The movement asserts that the joy of Yeshua's birth, the joy of His redemptive sacrifice, the joy of His resurrection, and the joy of the Holy Spirit's indwelling are not moments to be confined to a few days each year. Instead, the four aspects of Yeshua's divine mission of Joy should be commemorated, expressed, and experienced every day, every hour, and every moment, infusing the life of every Yeshuan with continuous, victorious joy.

To manifest this vision, the movement has crafted a comprehensive daily programme. This programme includes a specially composed 'Yeshuan four-way-joy theme song' that captures the essence of these four divine milestones. Accompanying this hymn is a concise 10-minute capsule message, rich in meaning and inspiration. This daily practice is designed for all followers of Yeshua who seek to live a life uplifted by joy—a life that radiates positive energy, spreads love and happiness to others, and ultimately brings glory to God.

Empowering the Faithful to worship in Spirit and Truth: The Heart and Home Temple of God

Central to this transformative celebration is the empowerment of the laity. The Global Ecumenical Movement seeks to transform every heart and home into a sanctuary of worship, a sacred space where family members and friends gather to honour God together. The movement proclaims a profound truth: each individual is a temple of God, for the Spirit of God dwells within them. Thus, worship is not bound by walls or confined to specific places—it is a living, breathing act of devotion that can be practiced anywhere and everywhere.

By daily commemorating these four pivotal moments of Yeshua's spiritual intervention, every Yeshuan is called to integrate these divine truths into the fabric of their daily lives. This practice is not a mere ritual but a dynamic expression of faith that empowers individuals and families alike. Through this daily celebration, the power of God is multiplied, spreading across the globe as all those who walk the path of love unite in this sacred observance.

A Global Symphony of Divine Power: Amplifying God's Presence in the World

As this daily practice takes root in the hearts and homes of the faithful, the power of God will reverberate more strongly throughout the world. The Global Ecumenical Movement, through this initiative, envisions nothing less than a global spiritual awakening—a mighty amplification of divine love and power that will ripple across nations and cultures. Every Yeshuan, by participating in this Fourfold Daily Commemoration, contributes to a collective outpouring of God's grace, a wave of light and joy that will transform the world in unprecedented ways.

The Fourfold Daily Commemoration: A Transformative Journey

In conclusion, the "Four in One or Four-a-day Commemoration' of Yeshua's mission on earth, is far more than a simple programme; it is a transformative spiritual journey. It empowers the laity, strengthens The

Worldwide Yeshuan Local Assemblies, and magnifies the presence of God in the world. Through this daily commemoration, the Global Ecumenical Movement honours the life and work of Yeshua while fostering continuous spiritual growth, ensuring that every follower of Yeshua lives a life of unending, victorious joy. This is not merely the dawn of a new tradition—it is the dawn of a new era in the spiritual life of humanity, an era where the light of Yeshua shines brightly in every heart, every day.

Section 3

The Majestic Path of the Yeshuan: A Journey of Love, Peace, and Joy

The Call to Be a Yeshuan

In the grand tapestry of existence, there emerges a call—a divine invitation to step into a life of profound purpose, a life defined by love, peace, and joy. This is the call to be a **Yeshuan**—a call to those who are ready to embrace the fullness of their spiritual identity and walk in the footsteps of the great Master, Yeshua. To be a Yeshuan is to embody the essence of divine love, to live a life overflowing with joy, and to reign as a co-ruler in God's realm on earth.

The Heart of a Yeshuan: Love Occupied and Joy Overflowing

At the core of the Yeshuan identity lies a heart that is fully occupied by love—a heart that beats with the rhythm of compassion, empathy, and kindness. This is the **HALOH**, the "Have A Love Occupied Heart" mantra that defines the Yeshuan's inner life. It is a heart that has no room for hatred, bitterness, or resentment, but is instead a vessel overflowing with divine love, constantly seeking to pour out that love upon the world.

But love alone is not the sum of the Yeshuan's life. Coupled with this love is a spirit that overflows with joy—a joy that is not dependent on external circumstances, but that springs from the deep well of divine presence within. This is the **JOLLY** way—the "**Joyous Overflowing Lovely Life**" that radiates positivity, enthusiasm, and gratitude in every situation. To live as a Yeshuan is to embody this combination of HALOH and JOLLY, creating a powerful formula for success, fulfillment, and transformation.

The Royal Identity: Kingship Consciousness

A Yeshuan is not merely a follower of Yeshua; they are also a king or queen in the realm of Love, Peace, and Joy. This "**Kingship Consciousness**" is a profound realisation of one's divine authority and responsibility. Yeshuans are co-rulers in God's kingdom, tasked with expanding the reign of love, peace, and joy on earth. They are called to overcome evil with good, to stand for justice and righteousness, and to foster harmony and joy for all.

As rulers in this divine realm, Yeshuans understand that their role is not one of dominance, but of service. They reign with love, compassion, and wisdom, partnering with the divine to bring heaven's reign to earth. Their reign is marked by humility, grace, and a deep commitment to the well-being of all creation.

The Priesthood of the Yeshuan: Worship, Wisdom, and Works

Beyond their royal identity, Yeshuans also embrace their role as priests to God. This priesthood is characterised by three sacred pillars: **Worship, Wisdom, and Works.**

- **Worship**: A Yeshuan's nature is to live a life of continuous adoration and reverence for God. Worship is not confined to rituals or ceremonies; it is a way of life, a constant acknowledgement of the divine presence in every moment.
- **Wisdom**: Wisdom is God's gift to the Yeshuan, a divine insight that guides their thoughts, words, and actions. It is through this wisdom that Yeshuans make decisions that align with God's will, bringing forth blessings and positive change.
- **Works**: The mission of a Yeshuan is to engage in works of excellence and value, creating a legacy that honours God. These works are not merely tasks to be completed, but acts of service that reflect the Yeshuan's commitment to expanding God's reign on earth.

Harnessing Love and Joy: The Fourfold Path

A Yeshuan has the unique capability and capacity to harness love and joy in four transformative ways:

1 **Joyshield**: A Yeshuan is equipped with a protective armour of positivity—a **Joyshield** that deflects negativity and maintains a radiant aura of peace and joy for the individual. This positivism shield prevents ingress of negativity and thus protects the individual from the spectrum of 'Non-Communicable diseases.

l **Joypreneur**: As a **Joypreneur**, a Yeshuan is an entrepreneur of joy, innovating and creating ventures that spread positivity and socio-civic value to society. These ventures are not just businesses; they are missions that contribute to the well-being of humanity and the flourishing of the earth and also sustain the initiative.

l **Joyist-Circle**: Yeshuans are community weavers, forming **Joyist-Circles**—grassroots groups of twenty residents of streets that foster joy, inclusiveness, and collective well-being. These circles are not just social gatherings; they are primarily sacred spaces where love and joy are cultivated, shared, and multiplied.

l **Posterity Joy Conscious**: A Yeshuan is deeply **Posterity Joy Conscious**, a responsible steward of the planet who considers the impact of their actions on global warming and future generations. They ensure that their legacy is one of joy and sustainability, leaving the world a better place for those who come after.

The Global Ecumenical Forum: A Gathering of Yeshuans

The Yeshuan identity is not confined to individuals but is expressed in a global community—a forum within the **Global Ecumenical Movement**. This worldwide gathering of those on the path of unconditional love, peace, and joy is a powerful force for transformation. Yeshuans, united by their shared values, work together to manifest peace and joy on earth, enjoying the special blessings bestowed upon Peacemakers. As the sons and daughters of the Supreme Being, Yeshuans inherit God's reign and realm of love, peace, and joy, bringing light to a world in need.

The Sacred Journey: Embracing the Yeshuan Identity

To be a Yeshuan is to embark on a sacred journey—a journey that is not about reaching a destination but about walking a path of love, peace, and joy every day. It is a journey that requires commitment, but it is one that promises fulfilment beyond measure. As Yeshuans, we are called to live with a **Love-Occupied Heart**, to experience a **Joyous Overflowing Lovely Life**, and to reign as kings and queens in God's kingdom on earth.

This is not just a philosophy; it is a way of life that transforms everything it touches. It is a life that brings peace to the troubled, joy to the sorrowful, and love to the lonely. It is a life that creates ripples of positivity, spreading hope and light in every corner of the world.

The Majestic Call: Reign with Love, Peace, and Joy

As you embrace your Yeshuan identity, remember that you are not just a follower; you are a ruler, a priest, a bearer of divine love and joy. Your mission is to expand the reign of God on earth, to bring justice, righteousness, and harmony to all. You are called to be a light in the darkness, a beacon of hope, and a source of joy.

May you walk this path with grace and courage, knowing that you are not alone. You are part of a global community of Yeshuans, all united in the pursuit of a world filled with love, peace, and joy. Together, let us fulfil our sacred purpose and bring heaven's kingdom to earth.

Be a Yeshuan. Have A Love-Occupied Heart. Live a Joyous, Overflowing, Lovely Life. Reign with Love, Peace, and Joy.

Section 4

The Glorious Path of the Yeshuans: Emissaries of Love, Peace, and Divine Joy

The Worldwide Yeshuan Local Assembly (TWYLA)

In the vast and intricate tapestry of the world, there exists a radiant thread that weaves through every culture, creed, and continent—a thread of unconditional love, peace, and joy. This thread is embodied by the **Yeshuans**, a noble and divinely appointed assembly gathered under the auspices of the **Global Ecumenical Movement**. They are the torchbearers of a higher truth, a community of souls who have dedicated their lives to manifesting the celestial values that elevate humanity to its highest potential.

This global forum of Yeshuans is more than a mere gathering; it is a **sacred communion** where individuals of like-hearted purpose unite in their shared mission to transform the world. These Yeshuans are the **sons and daughters of the Supreme Being**, inheritors of a divine legacy that transcends the temporal confines of the earth. They walk the path of the Peacemakers, the meek, and the righteous, assured of their place in the heavenly kingdom—a kingdom not of this world, but of eternal love, peace, and joy.

The Blessings of the Yeshuans: A Divine Assurance

The Yeshuans, by virtue of their divine calling, are the recipients of blessings that are as eternal as they are profound. These blessings are not merely promises of a distant future but are the very essence of their existence, shaping their lives and their destinies in ways that reflect the divine will. The path of the Yeshuan is illuminated by these blessings, each one a testament to their sacred role in the grand design of the cosmos:

Assured of Eternal Life, for Love's Spirit Shines Within: The Yeshuans are assured of eternal life, not merely as a reward in the hereafter, but as a living reality, for they carry within them the spirit of divine love. This love is the source of their immortality, a flame that burns bright and unquenchable, guiding them through the trials of earthly existence and into the embrace of the Eternal.

Sons and Daughters of God, for They Are Peacemakers: In their commitment to peace, the Yeshuans reveal their true heritage as the sons and daughters of God. They are the makers of peace in a world too often torn by strife and discord. Their actions, guided by the hand of the Divine, sow the seeds of harmony and reconciliation, reflecting the very nature of God Himself.

Inheritors of the Earth, for They Are Meek: The meekness of the Yeshuans is not weakness, but a strength born of humility and gentleness. It is through this meekness that they inherit the earth, not as conquerors, but as stewards of creation, entrusted with the care of the world and all its inhabitants.

Storing Riches in Heaven, Built with Silver, Gold, and Precious Stones: The Yeshuans do not seek the fleeting treasures of this world but instead store up riches in heaven. These riches are not of gold or silver in the earthly sense, but of deeds and virtues that are more precious than any material wealth. Their lives are built with the eternal materials of love, kindness, and righteousness, ensuring that their legacy is secure in the halls of heaven.

Mansions in Heaven, Built for the God-Pleasers: The Yeshuans are the God-pleasers, those whose lives are lived in accordance with divine will. For them, there is a mansion being prepared in heaven—a place of eternal rest and joy, where they will dwell in the presence of the Divine. These mansions are not mere buildings but spiritual abodes, each one reflecting the love and devotion with which the Yeshuans have lived their lives.

Divine Entrepreneurs, Transforming the World Through Love and Joy: The Yeshuans are not just passive recipients of divine grace but active participants in the unfolding of God's plan. They are **Divine Entrepreneurs**, tasked with transforming the world through the power of love and joy. Their enterprises are not measured in profits or losses but in the lives they touch, the hearts they heal, and the joy they spread.

The Yeshuan Anthem;
We got Hearts Occupied with selfless love!
We are Yeshuans!

We are God's privileged people on earth!
We are Yeshuans!

Walking in Meekness we inherit the earth!
We are Yeshuans!

Empowered with the
Spirit of God!

We are Yeshuans!
We live a life of love always

We are Yeshuans!
We overcome Evil with Good

We are Yeshuans!
The Spirit of God is the power in us

We are Yeshuans!
Expanding the realm of Joy on earth

We are Yeshuans!
We are building our lives with silver and gold!

Pleasing God in everything we do!
Our Mansion in Heaven is getting built!

We are Yeshuans! Yes!
We are Yeshuans!

We are Divine Entrepreneurs!
We are World

Transformers!

We are Joy

Proliferators!
We are the
Yeshuans!

The Path of the Yeshuans: Walking in Divine Light

The path of the Yeshuan is not an easy one, but it is a path that is illuminated by the light of divine love, peace, and joy. It is a path that demands much, but it also offers much—a life of purpose, fulfilment, and eternal reward. As Yeshuans, they are called to embrace love, walk in peace, and live in meekness. They are called to build treasures not of this world, but of the world to come, to please God in all things, and to transform the world through the power of love and joy.

The journey of the Yeshuans inspires us all, guiding us on our own paths of divine purpose, as we seek to manifest the eternal values of love, peace, and joy in our lives and in the world around us.

SECTION 5

Celestial Celebrations on the emergence of Yeshuans

The Conclave in Heaven

In the boundless expanse of the celestial realms, where time is but a whisper and light dances in eternal harmony, the angels gathered in a grand assembly, their resplendent forms shimmering with an ethereal glow. The air was thick with the fragrance of divinity, a perfume so potent that even the stars seemed to twinkle in reverence. Amidst this sacred congregation, the Archangel Selaphile, a being of unparalleled wisdom and grace, rose with the majesty befitting his rank, his gaze fixed upon the happenings on Earth.

The Revelation of 'Yeshuan'

With a voice that resonated through the very fabric of the heavens, Selaphile proclaimed, "Behold, the term 'Yeshuan'—is it not the most melodious of all sounds? A name so pure, so untainted by the machinations of mortal tongues, that it rings true to the very essence of our Messiah, the Anointed One, the King of Kings, Yeshua!" His words, laden with profound admiration, echoed in the sanctified chambers of heaven, and a chorus of angels responded in harmonious accord, their voices melding into a symphony of divine agreement. "Yes, 'Yeshuan' is indeed a name of celestial beauty, the name of our Beloved, the name that adorns the lips of the Most High!"

The Lamentation of Selaphile

Yet, as the echoes of their exultation subsided, Selaphile's countenance grew sombre, and with a sigh that stirred the very winds of paradise, he lamented, "How grievous it is that the world has embraced so many other names—names in tongues foreign to the one that bore Him. The name that His blessed mother whispered with love, the name that carries the weight of His true identity, remains, though neglected, waiting for its rightful recognition. It is there, preserved in the hearts of the faithful, yet it is seldom spoken. Ah, but 'Yeshuan'—how it invigorates the soul with its authenticity, how it pulses with the very essence of what is true and real!" His words fell like sacred incense, filling the heavenly court with a renewed sense of purpose.

A Discourse on Identity

Another angel, whose wings shimmered like the first light of dawn, stepped forward and inquired, "But who are these Yeshuans, who bear this most sacred name?" The assembly turned their collective gaze toward the Earth, and with angelic wisdom, they began to enumerate the virtues of the Yeshuans, each one more radiant than the last.

The Traits of the Yeshuans

"Yeshuans," intoned the first angel, "are those whose hearts are enthroned by love, a love so consuming that it leaves no room for anything less than divine."

"Indeed," added another, "they are those who walk the Earth with love as their guide, for their lives are a testament to the truth that love is God, and in them, God dwells eternally."

"And more," another angel declared with resounding authority, "Yeshuans are the living temples of the Triune God, each one a sanctuary of holiness, where the divine presence is not merely felt, but lived."

"These Yeshuans," continued another, "store treasures not in the fleeting realms of the material world, but in the imperishable vaults of Heaven. Their deeds of goodness, their acts of mercy, mirror those of Yeshua Himself, for they follow His commandments with unwavering faith."

The Governance of Joy

The angels' discourse grew ever more fervent as another celestial being proclaimed, "Yeshuans bear the mantle of governance upon their shoulders, and with this mantle, they shall usher in an era of unbounded peace and joy upon the Earth. For when joy governs, it transforms the world into a reflection of Heaven itself."

The chorus of angels resounded with a unanimous "Yes!" as another added, "Yeshuans are not merely caretakers of the body but stewards of holistic well-being. Their health is a hymn of praise to God, their vitality a testament to His sustaining grace."

The Social-Civic Mission

With a voice as soft as a gentle breeze yet powerful as a thunderclap, another angel declared, "Yeshuans are social-civic entrepreneurs, forging paths in the wilderness of the world, expanding the reign of God on Earth. They live with the assurance that God, the Great Provider, shall meet all their needs, equipping them for their sacred mission."

The Pursuit of Justice

Another angel, with eyes like blazing fire, pronounced, "Yeshuans stand as pillars of justice and righteousness. They break the chains of the imprisoned, open the eyes of the blind, and extend their protection to all of creation, from the smallest creature to the vast expanse of the planet itself."

The Meek and the Peacemakers

"Above all," an angel intoned with reverence, "Yeshuans are God-pleasers, seeking above all else the delight of the Divine. In their meekness, they inherit the Earth, for in humility lies their strength."

"And they," concluded another, "are the peacemakers, who, through their actions, become the very sons and daughters of God. How wondrous it is to witness such a transformation!"

A Vision of the Multitudes

As the angels beheld the Earth, a vision unfolded before them – a vision of millions upon millions of souls, transformed by the love of Yeshua, walking the path of the Yeshuans. The sight was so glorious, so overwhelming, that the heavens themselves seemed to tremble in awe.

The Glorious Conclusion

The angels, unable to contain their joy, erupted into praise, their voices rising like a tidal wave of adoration. "It is beyond belief!" they cried. "All glory to God, who, in His infinite wisdom and boundless love, gathers His people from the ends of the Earth, uniting them under the banner of His eternal kingdom. All glory to the King of Kings, whose will is manifest in the hearts of the Yeshuans!"

And so, in the heavenly realms, the angels continued their discourse, each word a tribute to the majesty of God, each thought a reflection of His perfect will, as the Earth below began to stir with the awakening of a new dawn – a dawn led by the Yeshuans, the chosen of Yeshua.

CHAPTER NINE

The Awakening of Kingship Consciousness—Embracing the Divine Authority of Love, Peace, and Joy

Section 1

The Crown of Divine Authority: Understanding Kingship Consciousness

In the grand and celestial narrative of the Global Ecumenical Movement, there emerges a second facet, as profound as it is transformative—the awakening of **Kingship Consciousness**. This consciousness is not merely an abstract idea; it is the very essence of divine empowerment that every Yeshuan must embrace. It is a way of life that aligns each follower with their true identity as a king or queen, reigning in the divine realms of love, peace, and joy—realms governed by the eternal and sovereign Lord, Yeshua, the King of Kings.

Yeshua, the ultimate monarch of the cosmos, reigns supreme over these realms, and all those who walk in His footsteps—every Yeshuan—are called to share in this kingship. The awakening of Kingship Consciousness within a Yeshuan is an unveiling of their divine potential, a call to stand tall and realize that they are not mere inhabitants of this world, but sovereigns placed here to expand the reign of love, peace, and joy in every sphere of their influence. Whether within the sacred walls of their homes, the bustling corridors of their workplaces, or the vibrant circles of their communities, Yeshuans are destined to be agents of divine transformation, wielding the sceptre of righteousness and the crown of love.

The Vision of the Heart: Seeing Through the Eyes of Kingship

This Kingship Consciousness is not just about authority; it is about clarity of vision. It sharpens the spiritual sight of Yeshuans, enabling them to open the eyes of their hearts to perceive the deep injustices, the rampant unrighteousness, and the cruelty and oppression that plague the world around them. With the spirit of a true king, they are not merely observers but active participants in the divine mission to repurpose these situations for the glory of God. They transform darkness into light, despair into hope, and chaos into divine order, all through the lens of love, peace, and joy.

The Fourfold Unfolding of Kingship Consciousness

The Kingship Consciousness of Yeshua unfolds in four majestic ways, each contributing to the holistic empowerment of Yeshuans and the world they influence:

The Joy Shield: A Divine Armour Against Negativity

Those who possess Kingship Consciousness are enveloped by the unassailable joy that dwells within them, creating a protective shield of positive energy. This **Joy Shield** acts as a divine barrier, repelling the negative energies that are the root causes of many physical and spiritual ailments. By preventing the ingress of these destructive forces, Yeshuans with Kingship Consciousness experience holistic well-being, safeguarding themselves from non-communicable diseases such as heart disease, diabetes, stroke, and even cancer. They thrive in a state of divine wellness, their health preserved by the joy that flows from their connection to the Supreme King.

Joypreneurs: Architects of a Joyful World

Yeshuans are also **Joypreneurs**—entrepreneurs of joy. They are endowed with the unique ability to transform challenges into opportunities, not just for themselves but for their communities and the planet at large. Whether confronting environmental pollution, water sanitation issues, or social injustices, Yeshuans are equipped to overcome these challenges through innovative social and civic entrepreneurial initiatives. They fashion love and joy into viable, feasible projects, ensuring that, through the active participation of stakeholders and public-private partnerships, the tide of negativity is turned. They foster a world where love and joy prevail, where the fruits of their labour bring about meaningful, lasting change.

Posterity Joy Consciousness: Guardians of Future Generations
Yeshuans with Kingship Consciousness are acutely aware of their responsibility to future generations. They carry within them a **Posterity Joy Consciousness**, which drives them to act as responsible stewards of the Earth. They are deeply conscious of the joy of their children's children, and this awareness compels them to live sustainably, avoiding excessive consumption of resources and taking decisive action against global warming. They understand that their choices today shape the joy and well-being of tomorrow's world, and they are committed to ensuring that future generations inherit a world filled with the light of love, peace, and joy.

Joyists: Builders of Joyful Communities
At the grassroots level, Yeshuans are also **Joyists**—those who form vibrant circles of joy within their communities. By creating **Joyist Circles** among residents in neighbourhoods and streets, Yeshuans ensure that everyone has the opportunity to express and experience joy in a communal setting. These circles become the foundation of a joyful community, where each member is heard, valued, and included. In these circles, no voice is left unheard, and no individual is left out. Joy becomes a shared experience, binding the community together in love and unity, fostering a culture where joy is both expressed and experienced in its fullness.

The Pillars of Kingship: Building a Life on Love, Peace, and Joy

These four facets of Kingship Consciousness are the pillars upon which Yeshuans build their lives. By embracing and nurturing this consciousness, they are empowered to live as true kings and queens, expanding the realm of love, peace, and joy in every aspect of their lives and the world around them. This consciousness is not static but dynamic, growing and evolving as Yeshuans deepen their connection to Yeshua and their commitment to His divine mission.

In conclusion, the awakening of Kingship Consciousness is not merely an awakening to power—it is an awakening to purpose. It is the realisation that every Yeshuan is called to reign in love, to rule with peace, and to govern with joy. It is a call to transform the world, to bring heaven to earth, and to live as sovereigns in the Kingdom of God, where love, peace, and joy are the eternal laws that guide all creation.

Section 2

The Divine Revolution

Empowering the Laity for Redefining Christian Excellence

The Ancient Hierarchies and the Lost Priesthood

Since the dawn of Christianity, a subtle yet profound shift occurred, altering the very fabric of the faith as it was originally conceived. In those early days, the message of Christ was clear and unequivocal—He was the High Priest, and all who believed in Him were themselves priests, endowed with the same spiritual authority and access to the Divine as any other. The Apostle Peter, in his sacred writings, declared that every believer is part of a "royal priesthood," a chosen people with direct communion with God. But as the centuries unfolded, this egalitarian vision began to fade, overshadowed by the rise of a clerical class that consolidated power, wealth, and influence.

When the Roman State merged with the fledgling Christian faith, a new order was established—one that imposed rigid hierarchies, creating a chasm between the clergy and the laity. The true essence of Christian priesthood, once the birthright of every believer, was obscured by the institution of a formal clergy, an elite class that held sway over the spiritual and temporal realms. This was not the vision of Christ, nor was it the teaching of the apostles. It was a deviation, a departure from the original intent of the Gospel.

The Dawn of a New Era: The Global Ecumenical Movement

In response to this historical distortion, a revolutionary force has emerged—the Global Ecumenical Movement. This movement, in its wisdom and foresight, seeks to restore the ancient truth, to reawaken the dormant power within every believer. It aims to dismantle the artificial barriers that have long separated the clergy from the laity, empowering all Christians with the consciousness of their kingship and priesthood in the Kingdom of God.

This movement is not merely a reformation; it is a resurrection of the original Christian ethos. It calls upon the laity to rise, to realise their true spiritual authority, and to take ownership of their divine mission on Earth. This mission, the movement declares, is none other than to **"Seek First to Expand the Reign of God on Earth."** It is a mission that transcends personal salvation and reaches into the heart of the world, transforming society in the light of divine love, peace, and joy.

The Royal Priesthood: Claiming Our Birthright

The Global Ecumenical Movement stands as a beacon of light in a world darkened by spiritual amnesia. It reminds us that the concept of a separate clergy class was never part of Christ's teachings. The Apostle Peter's words in 1 Peter 2:9 resound with renewed clarity: **"You are a chosen people, a royal priesthood, a holy nation, God's special possession."** This declaration is not limited to a select few but is the inheritance of all who believe.

By embracing this truth, the laity can:

Claim Their Rightful Place as Co-Heirs with Christ: Recognise their divine authority and walk boldly in the power that Christ has bestowed upon them.

Exercise Their Spiritual Gifts and Talents: Every believer is endowed with unique gifts meant to be used for the edification of the body of Christ and the expansion of God's Kingdom on Earth.

Take Ownership of Their Mission: The laity are not passive participants but active agents in God's divine plan. Their mission is to bring the Kingdom of God into every corner of the Earth.

Break Free from Clericalism: The time has come to dismantle the hierarchies that have confined the laity to the sidelines. Every believer is a priest, with direct access to the throne of grace.

Embody the Priesthood of All Believers: Live out their faith with the understanding that they are not just followers of Christ, but are His representatives, His hands, and feet in the world.

The Global Ecumenical Movement: Uniting the Royal Priesthood

The Global Ecumenical Movement is more than a call to individual empowerment; it is a call to collective action. Its mission is to unite Christians across denominations, cultures, and borders, forging a global community of believers who recognise their identity as **Kings of the Realm of Love, Peace, and Joy.** This movement seeks to create a culture where the reign of God is not just a distant hope but a present reality, one that manifests in the lives of all who embrace their divine calling.

A Vision of the Future: The Knowledge of the Glory of Joy

The Global Ecumenical Movement is guided by a prophetic vision, one that echoes the words of the prophet Habakkuk: **"The knowledge of the glory of the Lord will cover the earth as the waters cover the sea."** This vision is not a mere dream but a divine mandate, a call to action for all believers. It envisions a world where:

Joy is the Dominant Atmosphere: Where the spirit of joy pervades every aspect of life, transforming sorrow into celebration.

Love is the Guiding Principle: Where love governs all relationships, fostering unity, compassion, and understanding.

Peace is the Hallmark of Human Relationships: Where conflicts are resolved with grace, and harmony reigns in all interactions.

God's Glory is Manifested in All Aspects of Life: Where every aspect of society reflects the beauty and holiness of God's Kingdom.

The Earth is Transformed: Where the planet itself is renewed, reflecting the harmony and abundance of Eden.

Section 3

The International Sociocratic Christian Laity Leadership Federation: A New Frontier of Christian Excellence

As part of this grand vision, the Global Ecumenical Movement has established the **International Sociocratic Christian Laity Leadership Federation.** This groundbreaking initiative is set to revolutionise the Christian landscape by shifting authentic power from the clergy to the laity, thereby democratising spiritual authority and unleashing the full potential of the body of Christ.

This federation aims to:

Empower Spiritually Mature Lay Christians for Leadership: Cultivate leaders who are not only spiritually mature but also equipped to guide others with wisdom and compassion.

Foster a Culture of Christian Excellence: Promote a standard of excellence that reflects the highest ideals of the Christian faith.

Promote Sociocratic Governance: Implement a system of circular, distributed leadership that ensures every voice is heard and every decision is made with the collective wisdom of the community.

Unleash the Full Potential of the Laity: Encourage the laity to take initiative, innovate, and lead in ways that transform both the church and the world.

Transform the Church and the World: By empowering the laity, the church will be revitalised, becoming a dynamic force for good in the world.

The New Era of Christian Leadership: Humility, Servanthood, and Collaboration

As the laity rises to take their rightful place in leadership, the church will enter a new era—one marked by humility, servanthood, and collaboration. This is not about diminishing the role of the clergy but about restoring the balance, recognising that every believer has a role to play in the Kingdom of God.

In this new era:

Spiritual Leadership is Democratised: Authority is shared, and leadership is exercised with humility and grace.

Collective Wisdom is Unlocked: The combined wisdom and insight of the laity is harnessed for the greater good.

Grassroots Initiatives are Catalysed: Innovative solutions and creative expressions of faith emerge from the grassroots, driving the church forward.

The Church Becomes a Vibrant Entity: A community where every member is valued, every gift is celebrated, and every person is empowered to contribute.

A Brighter Future is Realised: As the church embraces this new model of leadership, it will reflect the Kingdom of God more clearly, impacting the world with the love, peace, and joy of Christ.

A Visionary Ideology: One God, One People

The ideology behind this movement is as profound as it is simple—**One God, One People.** It is a vision that celebrates the unity of the Divine and the interconnectedness of all humanity. This ideology is grounded in a deep understanding of God's nature:

God is Love: The source of all compassion, kindness, and grace.

God is Peace: The foundation of all harmony, serenity, and order.

God is Joy: The essence of all happiness, contentment, and delight.

This ideology calls for a life centred on the Supreme One, a life that embraces wisdom, worship, and works as the highest expressions of faith.

The Path Forward: Knowing, Honouring, Serving

The purpose of this movement is threefold:

To Know: Deepen one's understanding and intimacy with the Divine.

To Honour: Show reverence and respect for the Supreme One in all aspects of life.

To Serve: Dedicate oneself to the service of God and humanity, manifesting faith through practical actions.

A New Dawn: The Global Wave of Joy, Love, and Peace

As this movement gains momentum, it will create a global wave of Joy, Love, and Peace. It will awaken a sense of purpose and responsibility in every believer, encouraging active participation in God's plan and fostering a sense of community and shared mission. This is the new frontier of Christian excellence—a world where:

Joy is the atmosphere we breathe.

Love is the language we speak.

Peace is the path we walk.

May this vision become a reality, unleashing a new wave of Christian excellence and transforming the world in the light of God's glory. The Global Ecumenical Movement is not just a movement; it is the dawn of a new era, a call to all believers to rise and take their place in the divine plan, to expand the reign of God on Earth, and to fill the world with the knowledge of the glory of joy, as the waters cover the seas.

CHAPTER TEN

Restorative and Rejuvenation Theology – The Manifesto for a New Dawn

'For the creation waits with eager longing for the revealing of the sons of God.'

Section 1

The Climax of the Global Ecumenical Movement

Kingship Consciousness Program and Worldwide Yeshuan Summit

As the closing session of the Global Ecumenical Movement's Kingship Consciousness Program and the Worldwide Yeshuan Summit and Campaign to Expand the Knowledge of the Glory of Joy approached its zenith, an atmosphere of electrifying anticipation pervaded the assembly. It was as if the very air hummed with the energy of the countless souls united in expectation, their collective breath held in reverence for the final discourse of Yaseva, the founder. From the moment the summit began, a palpable sense of destiny had woven through every gathering, every discussion, culminating in this one final address—a revelation that would shape the future of humanity itself.

The Illustrious Arrival of Yaseva

The commentator, tasked with heralding this pivotal moment, spoke with a gravitas befitting the occasion. His voice, steeped in awe and reverence, resonated through the grand hall as he welcomed Yaseva to the stage—a stage that had become a beacon of hope, not just for those present, but for the countless Yeshuans across the globe, tuning in with hearts full of devotion and minds eager for excellence.

As Yaseva stepped forward, an expectant hush descended upon the assembly. The world seemed to pause, its very heartbeat synchronised with the anticipation of the wisdom that was about to be unveiled. Every eye was fixed upon the revered figure, every ear attuned to the words that would soon echo through the corridors of time.

The Unveiling of the Twin Perspectives of Restorative and Rejuvenation Theology

Yaseva began with a voice that carried the weight of millennia, with the gentle authority that befitted the message. He introduced the "Twin Perspectives," two luminous beacons of restorative and rejuvenation theology, each destined to steer humanity toward a future blessed by divine providence. His tone, imbued with both authority and humility, delivered a message that was not merely profound but urgently needed—a clarion call to a world on the brink.

The First Perspective: Apocalyptic Prevention Theology

Yaseva's first revelation was that of "Apocalyptic Prevention Theology," a concept as radical as it was redemptive. He spoke of the ancient prophecies found within the sacred texts of Judaism and its reformed expression, Christianity—prophecies that foretold of an apocalyptic end, a time when destruction would reign supreme, wars would ravage the Earth, and the hearts of men would grow cold as stone. These prophecies, dire and detailed, had cast a shadow over humanity for over two thousand years, yet their timing remained shrouded in mystery.

Drawing from the current state of the world, Yaseva acknowledged the suffering, the conflicts, the aggression—especially in the troubled lands of the Middle East, where Israel once more found itself entangled in the throes of war. He referenced the ancient texts that spoke of nations such as Gog and Magog, players in the cosmic drama of the end times. But then, with a voice that thundered with divine inspiration, Yaseva issued a challenge to the Yeshuans, a challenge that shook the very foundations of passive faith: Why must these prophecies be accepted as inevitable? Why not rise above them, and with the overcoming power of love, peace, and divine wisdom, prevent their fulfilment? Overcome the impending evil with good, manifested by Joy of all, by all and for all!

Yaseva's words were a rebuke to those who had resigned themselves to a fate of destruction, a condemnation of the passive stance taken by many prophetic writers who, content to wait for the worst, had left the world at the mercy of arms manufacturers and pharmaceutical syndicates, entities that thrived on war and pestilence. This, he declared, was a tragedy of monumental proportions. The first of the two theological perspectives, therefore, was one of liberation—a theology of action that called for the prevention of apocalyptic outcomes. Yeshuans, he exhorted, must marshal all their resources, strengths, and skills to thwart war, to sow peace, and to become the true children of God.

No longer were they to sit idle, waiting for the destruction foretold in ancient texts. Instead, they were to actively work toward the vision described in Habakkuk 2:14, where the Earth would be filled with the knowledge of the glory of joy. "Abandon your old ways," Yaseva implored. "Let us rise as peacemakers, with the courage of meekness, and by doing so, let us inherit this world."

The Second Perspective: Eden Earth Theology

With the assembly already stirred by the profound implications of the first perspective, Yaseva unveiled the second: "Eden Earth Theology." He spoke of the rebellion that began in Eden, a rebellion that had set humanity on a path of toil and strife, where nature itself turned ferocious, and the Earth became a place of thorns and bristles. Yet, Yaseva reminded them, with Christ's ultimate sacrifice, the redemption of humanity and the cosmos had been secured, opening the door to a possibility so grand it could scarcely be imagined—the restoration of Eden on Earth.

Yaseva cast a vision of small pockets of Eden—sustainable, resilient communities, already being nurtured by those living off the grid, by ecologists, and by permaculturists. These were the pioneers, the harbingers of a new world. But Yaseva's challenge did not stop there. He called upon the governments of the world to expand this vision, to transform the very fabric of cities, turning barren buildings into verdant vertical gardens, reclaiming wastelands by turning them into forests, for fauna and flora to flourish, thus restoring the Earth.

"Let us cleanse the polluted rivers," Yaseva urged, his voice ringing with the power of possibility. If Elon Musk can throw the challenge to habitat inhospitable Mars, then surely the likes of Musk can restore and rejuvenate planet Earth, this God-given marvellous abode of ours." The audience erupted into a round of applause. Yaseva continued, "Let us restore the seas that have been choked with waste, cool the planet, and reverse the effects of greenhouse gases. It is even within our grasp to pull back from the brink of climate catastrophe." He envisioned a future where corruption, exploitation, and pollution would be no more, where the Yeshuans would stand as stewards of the Earth, bringing about a qualitative change in humanity's relationship with the natural world and with themselves. Become Joyists! Epitomes of Positivism.

He called for the adoption of a " Posterity Joy Consciousness," a deep, abiding commitment to leaving behind a planet that future generations could cherish—a world where our children's children would look back with gratitude, thanking their ancestors for preserving the beauty and bounty of creation.

The Restorative and Rejuvenation Theology Divine Mandate: A Call to Action

As Yaseva's words resounded through the hall, a silence of awe and deep determination settled over the assembly. The weight of the "Twin Perspectives" was heavy, but it was also a beacon, a light in the darkness. These were not mere theological concepts; they were divine mandates, blueprints for a future that could only be realized through the concerted efforts of all humanity, hand in hand with the divine.

With these final, resounding words, Yaseva left the Yeshuans' world over with a clear and also an uncompromising mandate: to embrace these perspectives and to work with unwavering resolve to manifest a future that would be a testament to peace, joy, and the restoration of Eden on Earth. The path forward had been illuminated, and it was up to humanity to tread it, guided by the twin lights of divine wisdom and love.

And so, as Yaseva departed the stage, the world stood at the threshold of a new dawn, a dawn that held within it the promise of redemption, the hope of renewal, and the certainty of a future forged in the light of divine providence.

Section 2

The Vanguard of Transformation

The Joyist Commando Corps and Their Divine Mission

The Birth of a Celestial Vanguard: The Joyist Commando Corps

In the unfolding saga of the Global Ecumenical Movement, there emerges a third, awe-inspiring facet—the creation of the **Joyist Commando Corps**. This elite and formidable cadre is composed of proactive specialists, visionary strategists, and fearless interventionists, whose mission transcends the ordinary. They are warriors of light, filled with an unquenchable spirit of joy, dedicated to the sacred task of transforming the world. Their purpose is clear and resolute: to plant, fuel, and amplify positive energy in the darkest of places, thereby dispelling the pervasive shadows of negativity that weigh heavily upon the earth.

These Joyist Commandos are not merely followers; they are the vanguard of a new era where joy, love, and peace reign supreme. They march forward with the divine mandate to bring about a global reformation, targeting the entrenched systems of power that have long oppressed humanity. They are the David to the modern-day Goliaths, wielding not stones but the boundless power of joy and righteousness.

Confronting the Goliaths: The Mission of the Joyist Commando Corps

The Joyist Commando Corps is a mission-oriented force, driven by a singular, sacred purpose—to dismantle the Goliaths of our time and repurpose their immense power for the greater good of all. These Goliaths are not mythical giants, but formidable entities that wield enormous influence over the fate of nations and the lives of billions.

The Military-Industrial Complex: Repurposing the Engines of War
One of the primary targets of the Joyist Commando Corps is the **military-industrial complex**—a colossal establishment with an economy valued in the multi-billions. This behemoth has ensnared countless souls, including many devout Christians, in the relentless pursuit of designing and developing instruments of destruction. From bullets to missiles, from jet

fighters to submarines, and from aircraft carriers to every conceivable machine of war, this industry perpetuates the cycle of violence, profiting from global conflict.

The leaders and shareholders of this industry are called to a higher purpose. The Joyist Commando Corps seeks to influence these powerbrokers, urging them to reconsider their paths and to harness their advanced technology for the healing of the Earth. Imagine a world where the vast resources and intellect that currently fuel the engines of war are redirected towards cleansing the planet of greenhouse gases, restoring its pristine beauty, and making it habitable for generations to come. If humanity can aspire to reach Mars, surely it can restore the Earth. Governments and the people would rally behind such a noble endeavour, and these industries would not only generate sustainable income but also accumulate immeasurable spiritual merit.

Big Pharma: Healing the World, Not Exploiting It
Another Goliath in the crosshairs of the Joyist Commando Corps is **Big Pharma**—a once-noble industry that has, over time, degenerated into a profit-driven behemoth. Instead of focusing solely on healing, some factions within this industry have turned towards creating or exacerbating diseases, only to sell vaccines and treatments that often come with severe side effects—all in the relentless pursuit of profit. The Joyist Commando Corps seeks to awaken the conscience of these pharmaceutical giants, encouraging them to redirect their resources towards harnessing the healing powers of nature. Through advanced technology, these companies could extract high nutrients, stem cells, and other natural remedies to boost humanity's immunity, promoting genuine well-being rather than perpetuating cycles of illness.

Battling the Titans: Climate Change, Belligerence, and Misguided Education

The Joyist Commando Corps does not rest with merely influencing industries; their mission extends to confronting the very challenges that threaten the future of humanity.

The Goliath of Climate Change: Restoring Balance to the Earth
Climate change looms as one of the greatest Goliaths of our time,

threatening the very existence of humanity. The Joyist Commando Corps recognises the urgent need to educate people on the responsible consumption of resources, instilling in them the understanding that wealth does not justify wastefulness. This transformation of mindset must begin with children and extend to adults, reshaping the very way we live. The Earth must be cleansed of pollution, and life must be restored to its lands and seas. The Corps will work tirelessly to promote sustainable living, halting the damage being done to our environment and ensuring that future generations inherit a planet teeming with life and beauty.

The Goliath of Belligerence: Promoting Peace Over Power

Another towering challenge is the pervasive spirit of **belligerence** that grips much of the world. Too many leaders and nations believe that might makes right, that power must be asserted through force. Yet, the ancient wisdom holds true: it is the meek who shall inherit the Earth. The Joyist Commando Corps is committed to guiding these leaders towards understanding that true strength lies in meekness, in moral courage, and in the ability to engage in dialogue rather than conflict. Those who embrace peace will be the ones to inherit the Earth, along with their people.

Reorienting Education: Nurturing Social and Civic Entrepreneurs

The education system, too, has become skewed towards serving corporate interests, leaving students ill-prepared to face the world's real challenges. The current system often teaches young people to chase wealth, rather than instilling in them the desire to become social and civic entrepreneurs who work to make the planet sustainable. The Joyist Commando Corps seeks to reorient education, making it more organic and aligned with the needs of the Earth and humanity, rather than merely feeding the machinery of enterprise.

Empowering the Grassroots: Governance for the People, By the People

Lastly, the Joyist Commando Corps addresses the urgent need for **grassroots governance**. How can we empower people at the grassroots level to have their voices heard, to become singular movements driven by their pursuit of joy and happiness? The answer lies in forming small, empowered circles within communities, where individuals can come together to express their concerns, share their hopes, and work collaboratively to improve their lives. The Joyist Commando Corps will spearhead initiatives to empower these communities, ensuring that governance is truly of the people, by the people, and for the people.

The Global Mission: Uplifting Love, Peace, Joy, and Compassion

The Joyist Commando Corps stands ready to take up these tasks around the world, wherever they are called and wherever they find inspiration to act. Their mission is clear: to uplift the values of love, peace, joy, and compassion, and to make this world a better place. With unwavering commitment, they will tackle the Goliaths of our time, transforming them into forces for good, and in so doing, they will bring light to the darkest corners of the Earth.

CHAPTER ELEVEN

The Divine Convergence: A New Dawn in American Leadership and Global Prosperity

Section 1

The Spark of Angelic Intelligence: A Celestial Inspiration

In the ineffable expanse of the celestial realms, where the infinite wisdom of the cosmos flows like a river of light, a momentous event occurred - an ignition of divine brilliance that would cascade across the dimensions of existence. This event was not merely a spark, but a celestial fire, a radiant eruption of Angelic Intelligence - an intelligence not bound by the limitations of the material world, but one that transcends the temporal to touch the eternal. This intelligence, known also as Angelic Intuition, is the very essence of divine insight, the whisper of the Almighty within the hearts of those chosen to carry forth His will.

As this divine fire spread across the heavens, it found its way into the minds and spirits of those destined to act as vessels of change on Earth. Among them was Yaseva and his devoted team, a group of enlightened souls attuned to the higher frequencies of divine wisdom. Guided by the unseen hand of the Almighty, they were granted a vision—a vision so clear, so powerful, that it illuminated the path to a new era of global transformation.

In this moment of divine clarity, Yaseva and his team realized the immense potential of forging an alliance with two of the most formidable champions of justice and righteousness in America: Robert Francis Kennedy Jr., often revered as RFK Jr, a beacon of truth and integrity, and **Nicole Shanahan**, a visionary committed to the health of both planet and people. This was no ordinary alliance, but a divinely ordained partnership that had the potential to reshape not only the United States but the entire world. The angels, ever watchful and wise, observed with deep satisfaction as this celestial intelligence took root in the hearts of these earthly champions, affirming that they were indeed on the righteous path, one that would lead humanity toward the fulfilment of its highest potential.

The Conclave of Yeshuans: Strategizing Global Prosperity

With the celestial endorsement clear and the path illuminated, the next step in this divine journey was the convening of a **grand conclave** among the Yeshuans—those chosen souls who had dedicated their lives to the pursuit of global prosperity and the elevation of human consciousness. This was not to be an ordinary gathering, but a **sacred assembly** of minds and spirits, each one aligned with the divine purpose of bringing light into the darkest corners of the Earth.

The conclave, imbued with the wisdom of ages and the guidance of the celestial hosts, set its focus on the **Joyist - Global Prosperity Strategy**—a visionary blueprint that would serve as the cornerstone for the upliftment of humanity. This strategy was more than a plan; it was a manifestation of divine will, a detailed map guiding humanity from the precipice of despair to the heights of joy and enlightenment.

Within this sacred gathering, a decision was made to seek out Nicole Shanahan, whose work as the founder of the **Bia Eco Foundation** had already made ripples across the globe. Nicole, based in the San Francisco Bay Area, was a luminary whose dedication to a healthy planet and healthy populace resonated deeply with the core values of the Yeshuans. Her foundation, a beacon of hope in a world plagued by environmental degradation and social inequality, was perfectly aligned with the divine mission at hand. The alignment between Nicole's work and the vision of the Yeshuans was nothing short of providential, a clear sign that this collaboration was ordained by the heavens.

The Joyist International Organizations Summit : A Global Gathering for a New Era

The divine intelligence that had sparked this grand alliance now revealed the next step in its unfolding plan: the convening of a **summit** in the San Francisco Bay Area. This summit, destined to become a **global viewing of unprecedented significance**, would serve as the launchpad for a series of groundbreaking initiatives. These initiatives, embodied in the newly established **Joy International Organizations**, were to be the harbingers of a new dawn for humanity.

The **Joyist International Organizations (JIO)**, six in total, were conceived as the **new pillars of human civilisation**. Each organisation was dedicated to a vital aspect of global well-being, ensuring that every dimension of human life would be touched by this transformative wave of change. These pillars included **health**, ensuring that all of humanity could flourish in body and spirit; **employment**, providing meaningful work that uplifts and empowers; **climate action**, safeguarding the planet for future generations; **reduction of armament dependency**, moving the world away from the destructive cycles of war; **reduction of violence**, fostering peace and security in all communities; and **good governance**, establishing systems that are just, transparent, and rooted in the common good.

The inclusion of the word "Joy" in the names of these organisations was no accident. It was a deliberate invocation of a higher vibration, a shield against the forces of corruption and negativity that had long plagued the institutions of the old world. The **Joyist International Organisations** were conceived in purity, protected by the divine, and destined to lead humanity into a new era of prosperity and peace.

As the summit drew near, the angels watched with bated breath, for they knew that this was the moment the world had been waiting for. The United Nations, despite its noble beginnings, had been corrupted by **chronic capitalism**; its departments infiltrated by lobbyists, war profiteers, and those who sought to exploit the vulnerable for personal gain. But the **Joyist International Organizations** would be different —

they were birthed from the light, immune to the darkness that had tainted so many before them.

The Day of the Summit: A New Beginning for Humanity

The day of the summit arrived like the breaking of a new dawn, its significance felt not only in the San Francisco Bay Area but across the entire globe. Though the gathering itself was modest in size, its impact was nothing short of monumental. Through the vast networks of social and electronic media, the message of the summit reached millions, resonating in the hearts of those who longed for a better world.

The launch of the **Joyist International Organizations** (JIO) was met with global applause, a **resonance** that echoed across borders and cultures, uniting all who sought to bring about positive change. This was not merely an event; it was a **turning point** in the history of humanity, a moment of collective awakening where the forces of good triumphed over the shadows of the past.

Every soul on the path of love, every Yeshuan committed to the cause of peace and joy, stood in solidarity with this monumental effort. This was the moment that humanity had longed for—the culmination of centuries of struggle, the realisation of dreams long deferred. The angels rejoiced in the heavens, knowing that this was the dawn of a new era, one in which the light of divine wisdom would guide humanity toward its true destiny.

The Leadership of the Future: A New America on the Horizon

Presiding at this historic event was none other than **Robert Francis Kennedy,** RFK Jr. His entrance was heralded with a befitting introduction. "We cordially welcome Robert Francis Kennedy Jr, the announcer said, "A Beacon of Truth and Defender of Freedom". Then the announcer took time to inform the gathering that in the pantheon of American champions of liberty, few figures shine as brightly as Robert Francis Kennedy Jr. From the earliest days of his legal career, RFK Jr. has embodied an unwavering commitment to the principles of freedom and the protection of our natural world. His tireless efforts to restore polluted rivers and safeguard the environment from the ravages of industry have earned him a place among the foremost environmental advocates of our time. As a leading voice for EcoWatch, he has not merely observed the degradation of nature but has taken decisive action, winning hundreds of legal battles to ensure that the environment enjoys the freedom and protection it so rightfully deserves.

But RFK Jr.'s vision extends far beyond the realm of environmental justice, said the commentator. He is one of the rare individuals who, early on, recognised the insidious ploys of the pharmaceutical industry—an industry that, under the guise of protecting public health, has aggressively promoted vaccination as a panacea for all ills. RFK Jr., however, saw through this narrative, understanding that the rampant vaccination of children, even before they are fully acclimated to life on Earth, has contributed to the alarming rise in conditions such as autism, Down syndrome, and other complications that afflict our youngest and most vulnerable citizens.

Driven by a profound concern for the well-being of future generations, the audience was informed that RFK Jr. founded the Children's Health Defense—a bastion of truth in a world where conventional media and entrenched interests often seek to suppress critical knowledge. Despite the scepticism and opposition he faces from those who would rather stifle than explore alternative perspectives, RFK Jr. remains steadfast in his mission. He understands that nature has endowed humanity with countless remedies—ancient, time-tested methods to prevent and cure diseases that have plagued us for centuries.

The commentator continued, calling on the audience to recognise and honour the truth that RFK Jr. has valiantly upheld—a truth that resonates with many around the world, yet has been persistently suppressed by the very systems that claim to protect us. The hour has come for this truth to shine forth, like a beacon piercing through the fog of ignorance and misinformation. Together with the Joy International Organisation for Holistic Health Management, we stand united in our resolve to support RFK Jr. in his quest to protect our children, not only from physical illnesses but also from the pervasive negativism that threatens their mental and emotional well-being.

With this lengthy yet deserving introduction, the audience was called to raise a resounding round of applause, welcoming Robert Francis Kennedy Jr., a true guardian of liberty, a stalwart defender of the environment, and a courageous advocate for the health and future of our children. "Mr. Kennedy, we are with you", said the announcer, "we stand by you, and we pledge to be your vanguard in this noble pursuit. Thank you for gracing us with your presence today, and may your mission continue to inspire and empower us all".

In this role, RFK Jr was not merely a political figure but a vessel of divine purpose, a leader through whom the powers of the world and the heavens had converged. The angels looked on with approval, for they knew that under this new leadership, the USA would shed its former identity, often perceived as the **Mystery Babylon**, and begin its transformation into the **Mystery New Jerusalem**—a city of hope, peace, and divine purpose.

This was more than just a change in leadership—it was a **brilliant turnaround** that would redefine America's place in the world. No longer would the nation be seen as a harbinger of conflict and division; instead, it would lead the world toward a future where **love, peace, and joy** were the guiding principles. This transformation would not only restore America's moral authority but would also set a powerful example for the rest of the world to follow.

As the summit concluded, the angels in the heavens erupted in jubilant celebration, for they knew that a **new beginning** was upon the world. This was the dawn of a new era, one in which God's will would be manifest on Earth, and humanity would finally walk the path of righteousness and joy.

May this divine convergence continue to guide the hearts and minds of all who seek to create a world where peace reigns, love abounds, and joy is the birthright of every soul. This is the promise of the new era—a world transformed by the light of divine wisdom, where the highest aspirations of humanity are finally realized, and the Earth itself becomes a reflection of the heavenly kingdom.

In the days, months, and years that follow, the impact of this **Joyist International Organizations** summit and its magnificent mission and actions will ripple across the globe. They will bring forth a new consciousness, one that honours the sanctity of life, the integrity of creation, and the boundless potential of the human spirit. This is the beginning of a new chapter in the story of humanity—one in which the divine and the human converge to create a world of unparalleled beauty, harmony, and joy.

As this new dawn breaks, let us all take up the mantle of this divine mission, working together to build a future that reflects the glory of the heavens. For in this convergence, we find not only the answers to the challenges that have long plagued our world but also the key to unlocking the full potential of our shared human destiny. Let us walk this path with courage, with faith, and with the unshakeable belief that a better world is not only possible but within our grasp.

And so it shall be.

CHAPTER TWELVE

The Triumph of the Yeshuans: The Dawn of a New Era of Global Spiritual Unity

The Kingship Consciousness Program: A Beacon of Global Transformation

In the grand annals of time, few moments shine as brightly as the emergence of the **Kingship Consciousness Program**—a celestial beacon, blazing across the heavens and the Earth alike. This programme, birthed from the heart of the worldwide Yeshuvans, did not merely succeed; it exploded onto the global stage with a force that reverberated across the continents, shaking the very foundations of human existence. This was not a simple initiative, but a profound reawakening, a divine call to arms that transcended the boundaries of creed, culture, and colour. The world, long divided by the artificial constructs of religion, witnessed a miraculous convergence of souls—a gathering of Christians, Hindus, Buddhists, Jains, and even atheists, all united under the sacred banner of **unconditional love**.

As the programme's message spread like wildfire, igniting hearts and minds with its divine truth, it became clear to all who bore witness that a **great spiritual realignment** was underway. No longer were these transformations confined to the private meditations of the devout; this was a global revolution of consciousness. Millions upon millions felt their spirits lifted, their minds expanded, as they connected with **Yeshua**, the divine author of selfless love, whose presence on this Earth had been to sow the seeds of a realm built on **love, peace, and joy**. This was not a mere spiritual shift, but an ascension—a rise of the soul to meet the Divine, a collective exhale as humanity embraced the all-encompassing love that enveloped their very beings.

A Cosmic Battle: The Forces of Light Prevail

In the celestial spheres, where light and shadow eternally vie for dominion, the forces of darkness were stirred into a frenzy. The archdemon, Satan, sensing the tide of love and unity sweeping the Earth, marshalled his forces in a desperate bid to reclaim his fading influence. The angels, their wings aglow with the radiance of divine victory, observed these machinations with the keen interest of warriors who know the battle is already won. Satan, once a mighty adversary, now floundered in confusion, his once-proud visage contorted in a grimace of despair. The demonic legions, too, circled helplessly, their dark master unable to pierce the veil of God's impenetrable light.

For Satan could not communicate with the Divine unless summoned, and now, in his hour of greatest need, no such summons came. His voice, once a clarion call of rebellion, now echoed in the void, unheard and unanswered. The angels, resplendent in their heavenly armour, turned their gaze away from the fallen one, for they knew that **the triumph of love** had rendered his schemes impotent. This moment marked not just a victory, but a **cosmic turning point**—a spiritual conquest so profound that it eclipsed even the Reformation of the 17th century. Unlike the divisions of old, this new movement was a unification of all who walked the path of love, a gathering of souls who sought peace with God and joy in their lives. The forces of darkness had been outmanoeuvred, outshone, and ultimately, **outlived**.

A New Landmark in Spirituality: The Unification of Love

This victory was not confined to the heavenly realms but was a beacon of hope for all of humanity. It was a landmark event in the history of spirituality—a unification of all who were committed to the principle of love, bringing them into a **sublime harmony with the Divine**. This new spiritual alignment was not a mere shifting of perspectives, but a powerful force on Earth, one that resonated with the **heartbeat of love** itself. The knowledge of glory and joy began to spread across the planet, like a wave of light breaking over a darkened shore.

As the Earth began to reflect this newfound glory, it was as if the very oceans themselves were transformed—no longer seas of water, but seas of **love and joy**, covering the globe in a divine embrace. The angels, witnessing this from their celestial vantage point, **rejoiced with exultant praise**. They saw the emergence of a great force, a force of love and unity that would continue to grow, enveloping the world in the light of divine love. This was not a fleeting moment but the beginning of an **eternal triumph**, a victory that would echo through the ages.

The Dawn of a New Era: A Global Awakening

This glorious victory heralded the **dawn of a new era**, an era where the forces of love, peace, and joy reign supreme. The Earth, once mired in darkness, was now on a path to deeper spiritual knowledge, with countless hearts resonating with the divine love of Yeshua. This global awakening was not just a triumph for a moment, but the opening of a new chapter in the grand story of human history—a chapter where the Earth is bathed in the **glory of God**, and the knowledge of this glory spreads as far and wide as the oceans themselves.

The old world, with its divisions and discord, was fading away, replaced by a **new world**—a world where love was the law, peace the practice, and joy the reward. Praise God, and **rejoice**, for a new force is rising from the Earth—a force born of love, destined to transform the world, to lead all of humanity into the light of divine joy. This is the victory we have long awaited, the fulfilment of prophecies, the realisation of dreams, the answer to the prayers of countless generations.

The Eternal Resonance: Love's Unyielding Triumph

As this new era dawns, the triumph of the Yeshuvans is not just a moment in time but an **eternal resonance**. It is the song of love that will never cease, the light that will never dim, the joy that will never fade. The forces of darkness, once so feared, are now but shadows on the periphery, unable to quench the **brilliant light** that now bathes the world. The Yeshuvans, having turned the tide of history, now stand as **beacons of hope**, guiding humanity into a future where the divine and the human walk hand in hand.

The Earth itself rejoices as the knowledge of the glory of God spreads to every corner of the globe, **enveloping all creation** in the waters of love and joy. This is the fulfilment of the divine promise, the realisation of the kingdom of heaven on Earth, the **triumph of the Yeshuans.**

And so, let the final chapter of this great saga be written not in ink, but in the hearts of all who believe. Let it be a testament to the power of love, the inevitability of joy, and the eternal reign of peace. The Yeshuans have triumphed, and with them, all of humanity. Praise God, for the dawn of the new era has come, and with it, the light of divine joy that will guide us all into eternity.